JB BLA

Brown, Jordan.

Elizabeth Blackwell /

LINDEN

ELIZABETH BLACKWELL

ELIZABETH BLACKWELL

JORDAN BROWN

CHELSEA HOUSE PUBLISHERS

NEW YORK • PHILADELPHIA

CHELSEA HOUSE PUBLISHERS
EDITOR-IN-CHIEF: Nancy Toff
EXECUTIVE EDITOR: Remmel T. Nunn
MANAGING EDITOR: Karyn Gullen Browne
COPY CHIEF: Juliann Barbato
PICTURE EDITOR: Adrian G. Allen
ART DIRECTOR: Maria Epes
MANUFACTURING MANAGER: Gerald Levine

American Women of Achievement
SENIOR EDITOR: Constance Jones

Staff for ELIZABETH BLACKWELL
TEXT EDITOR: Marian W. Taylor
ASSOCIATE EDITOR: Maria Behan
DEPUTY COPY CHIEF: Ellen Scordato
EDITORIAL ASSISTANT: Heather Lewis
PICTURE RESEARCHER: Toby Greenberg
ASSISTANT ART DIRECTOR: Laurie Jewell
DESIGN: Design Oasis
ASSISTANT DESIGNER: Donna Sinisgalli
PRODUCTION COORDINATOR: Joseph Romano
COVER ILLUSTRATOR: Vilma Ortiz

5   7   9   8   6   4

Library of Congress Cataloging-in-Publication Data

Brown, Jordan.
Elizabeth Blackwell / Jordan Brown.
p.   cm.—(American women of achievement)
Bibliography: p.
Includes index.
Summary: A biography of the first woman doctor, who paved
the way for other women entering the field of medicine.
ISBN 1-55546-642-7
      0-7910-0410-4 (pbk.)
1. Blackwell, Elizabeth, 1821–1910—Juvenile
literature.   2. Physicians—New York (State)—
Biography—Juvenile literature.   3. Women physicians—
New York (State)—Biography—Juvenile literature.
[1. Blackwell, Elizabeth, 1821–1910.   2. Physicians.
3. Women physicians.] I. Title.   II. Series.
R154.B623B76 1989   88-23584
610′.92′4—dc19   CIP
[B]   AC

CONTENTS

AMERICAN WOMEN of ACHIEVEMENT

Abigail Adams
women's rights advocate

Jane Addams
social worker

Louisa May Alcott
author

Marian Anderson
singer

Susan B. Anthony
woman suffragist

Ethel Barrymore
actress

Clara Barton
founder of the American Red Cross

Elizabeth Blackwell
physician

Nellie Bly
journalist

Margaret Bourke-White
photographer

Pearl Buck
author

Rachel Carson
biologist and author

Mary Cassatt
artist

Agnes De Mille
choreographer

Emily Dickinson
poet

Isadora Duncan
dancer

Amelia Earhart
aviator

Mary Baker Eddy
founder of the Christian Science church

Betty Friedan
feminist

Althea Gibson
tennis champion

Emma Goldman
political activist

Helen Hayes
actress

Lillian Hellman
playwright

Katharine Hepburn
actress

Karen Horney
psychoanalyst

Anne Hutchinson
religious leader

Mahalia Jackson
gospel singer

Helen Keller
humanitarian

Jeane Kirkpatrick
diplomat

Emma Lazarus
poet

Clare Boothe Luce
author and diplomat

Barbara McClintock
biologist

Margaret Mead
anthropologist

Edna St. Vincent Millay
poet

Julia Morgan
architect

Grandma Moses
painter

Louise Nevelson
sculptor

Sandra Day O'Connor
Supreme Court justice

Georgia O'Keeffe
painter

Eleanor Roosevelt
diplomat and humanitarian

Wilma Rudolph
champion athlete

Florence Sabin
medical researcher

Beverly Sills
opera singer

Gertrude Stein
author

Gloria Steinem
feminist

Harriet Beecher Stowe
author and abolitionist

Mae West
entertainer

Edith Wharton
author

Phillis Wheatley
poet

Babe Didrikson Zaharias
champion athlete

CHELSEA HOUSE PUBLISHERS

"Remember the Ladies"

MATINA S. HORNER

Remember the Ladies." That is what Abigail Adams wrote to her husband John, then a delegate to the Continental Congress, as the Founding Fathers met in Philadelphia to form a new nation in March of 1776. "Be more generous and favorable to them than your ancestors. Do not put such unlimited power in the hands of the Husbands. If particular care and attention is not paid to the Ladies," Abigail Adams warned, "we are determined to foment a Rebellion, and will not hold ourselves bound by any Laws in which we have no voice, or Representation."

The words of Abigail Adams, one of the earliest American advocates of women's rights, were prophetic. Because when we have not "remembered the ladies," they have, by their words and deeds, reminded us so forcefully of the omission that we cannot fail to remember them. For the history of American women is as interesting and varied as the history of our nation as a whole. American women have played an integral part in founding, settling, and building our country. Some we remember as remarkable women who—against great odds—achieved distinction in the public arena: Anne Hutchinson, who in the 17th century became a charismatic religious leader; Phillis Wheatley, an 18th-century black slave who became a poet; Susan B. Anthony, whose name is synonymous with the 19th-century women's rights movement, and who led the struggle to enfranchise women; and, in our own century, Amelia Earhart, the first woman to cross the Atlantic Ocean by air.

These extraordinary women certainly merit our admiration, but other women, "common women," many of them all but forgotten, should also be recognized for their contributions to American thought and culture. Women have been community builders; they have founded schools and formed voluntary associations to help those in need; they have assumed the major responsibility for rearing children, passing on from one generation to the next the values that keep a culture alive. These and innumerable other contributions, once ignored, are now being recognized by scholars, students, and the public. It is exciting and gratifying to realize that a part of our history that was hardly acknowledged a few generations ago is now being studied and brought to light.

In recent decades, the field of women's history has grown from obscurity to a politically controversial splinter movement to academic respectability, in many cases mainstreamed into such traditional disciplines as history, economics, and psychology. Scholars of women, both female and male, have organized research centers at such prestigious institutions as Wellesley College, Stanford University, and the University of California. Other notable centers for women's studies are the Center for the American Woman and Politics at the Eagleton Institute of Politics at Rutgers University; the Henry A. Murray Research Center for the Study of Lives, at Radcliffe College; and the Women's Research and Education Institute, the research arm of the Congressional Caucus on Women's Issues. Other scholars and public figures have established archives and libraries, such as the Schlesinger Library on the History of Women in America, at Radcliffe College, and the Sophia Smith Collection, at Smith College, to collect and preserve the written and tangible legacies of women.

From the initial donation of the Women's Rights Collection in 1943, the Schlesinger Library grew to encompass vast collections documenting the manifold accomplishments of American women. Simultaneously, the women's movement in general and the academic discipline of women's studies in particular also began with a narrow definition and gradually expanded their mandate. Early causes such as woman suffrage and social reform, abolition and organized labor were joined by newer concerns such as the history of women in business and the professions and in politics and government; the study of the family; and social issues such as health policy and education.

Women, as historian Arthur M. Schlesinger, jr., once pointed out, "have constituted the most spectacular casualty of traditional history. They have made up at least half the human race, but you could never tell that by looking at the books historians write." The new breed of historians is remedying that omission. They have written books about immigrant women and about working-class women who struggled for survival in cities and about black women who met the challenges of life in rural areas. They are telling the stories of women who, despite the barriers of tradition and economics, became lawyers and doctors and public figures.

The women's studies movement has also led scholars to question traditional interpretations of their respective disciplines. For example, the study of war has traditionally been an exercise in military and political analysis, an examination of strategies planned and executed by men. But scholars of women's history have pointed out that wars have also been periods of tremendous change and even opportunity for women, because the very absence of men on the home front enabled them to expand their educational, economic, and professional activities and to assume leadership in their homes.

The early scholars of women's history showed a unique brand of courage in choosing to investigate new subjects and take new approaches to old ones. Often, like their subjects, they endured criticism and even ostracism by their academic colleagues. But their efforts have unquestionably been worthwhile, because with the publication of each new study and book another piece of the historical patchwork is sewn into place, revealing an increasingly comprehensive picture of the role of women in our rich and varied history.

Such books on groups of women are essential, but books that focus on the lives of individuals are equally indispensable. Biographies can be inspirational, offering their readers the example of people with vision who have looked outside themselves for their goals and have often struggled against great obstacles to achieve them. Marian Anderson, for instance, had to overcome racial bigotry in order to perfect her art and perform as a concert singer. Isadora Duncan defied the rules of classical dance to find true artistic freedom. Jane Addams had to break down society's notions of the proper role for women in order to create new social institutions, notably the settlement house. All of these women had to come to terms both with themselves and with the world in which they lived. Only then could they move ahead as pioneers in their chosen callings.

Biography can inspire not only by adulation but also by realism. It helps us to see not only the qualities in others that we hope to emulate, but also, perhaps, the weaknesses that made them "human." By helping us identify with the subject on a more personal level they help us to feel that we, too, can achieve such goals. We read about Eleanor Roosevelt, for instance, who occupied a unique and seemingly enviable position as the wife of the president. Yet we can sympathize with her inner dilemma: an inherently shy woman, she had to force herself to live a most public life in order to use her position to benefit others. We may not be able to imagine ourselves having the immense poetic talent of Emily Dickinson, but from her story we can understand the challenges faced by a creative woman who was expected to fulfill many family responsibilities. And though few of us will ever reach the level of athletic accomplishment displayed by Wilma Rudolph or Babe Zaharias, we can still appreciate their spirit, their overwhelming will to excel.

A biography is a multifaceted lens. It is first of all a magnification, the intimate examination of one particular life. But at the same time, it is a wide-angle lens, informing us about the world in which the subject lived. We come away from reading about one life knowing more about the social, political, and economic fabric of the time. It is for this reason, perhaps, that the great New England essayist Ralph Waldo Emerson wrote, in 1841, "There is properly no history: only biography." And it is also why biography, and particularly women's biography, will continue to fascinate writers and readers alike.

ELIZABETH BLACKWELL

Elizabeth Blackwell, the first female physician of modern times, was 27 years old when she graduated from medical school in 1849.

ONE

"Doctrix Blackwell"

January 23, 1849, dawned clear and bright in Geneva, New York. As a brilliant sun warmed the air, more than a hundred young men, high-spirited and impatient, gathered outside the Presbyterian church on the Geneva Medical College campus. In a few moments, each would receive a diploma and a prestigious new title: *Doctor*. Wearing long black robes and flat tasseled hats, the students lined up behind a brass band for the commencement procession. One future graduate, however, stood apart.

Dr. James Webster, the college anatomy professor, suggested that the lone student join the other candidates. The answer was no. "Why not?" asked the doctor. "Because," said the doctoral candidate, "it wouldn't be ladylike."

Elizabeth Blackwell was the only woman in Geneva Medical College's class of 1849. She was also the only woman who had ever been admitted to medical school. She was about to become the only woman doctor in modern history. Her achievement had required courage, self-discipline, and the ability to ignore scornful criticism.

Blackwell possessed all these qualities, but she was still a 19th-century "lady," and ladies did not march in processions. Her aim was not to destroy society's conventions but to expand them, so that she and other like-minded women could follow their ambitions without becoming outcasts. She would, she told Webster primly, enter the church on the arm of her brother Henry, and she would sit quietly until her name was called during the ceremony.

After her two years of study in Geneva, Blackwell had become a familiar

Geneva Medical College (above, in an 1848 photograph) accepted Elizabeth Blackwell as a student in 1847. Twenty-eight other schools had rejected her.

sight to the townspeople, whose attitude toward her had ranged from curious to hostile. Women were particularly suspicious of this unconventional member of their sex. They stared and whispered when she walked through the town. What kind of female, they asked each other, would so openly defy tradition? How could a woman permit herself to share a classroom with men, hearing lectures about the human body and all its unmentionable aspects? "The theory was fully established," Blackwell recalled later, "either that I was a bad woman . . . or that, being insane, an outbreak of insanity would soon be apparent."

Whatever she was, Elizabeth Black-well fascinated the women of Geneva. Hours before the commencement, they had begun to assemble on the campus. Inside the church on this January morning, according to one spectator, nothing could be seen "but a vast expanse of women's bonnets and curious eyes." As Elizabeth and Henry Blackwell moved down the aisle, heads turned and murmurs filled the air. Henry Blackwell noticed the stir, but his deeply religious sister seemed oblivious to it. When she took her seat, she recalled afterward, she "gave one thought to friends, and then thought only of the Holy One." Seated at the front of the church was college president Benjamin Hale, who began to call out graduates' names. After 129 men had received their diplomas, Hale called the last student.

The spectators were silent as slender 27-year-old Elizabeth Blackwell approached the podium. Just over five feet tall, she wore her pale red-blond hair braided and coiled over her ears. Choosing not to wear the traditional robe of a graduate, she had bought a new black silk dress, trimmed at the cuffs and collar with white lace. She had hesitated about spending scarce money for this outfit, but, she joked later, she did not want to "disgrace womankind, the college, or the Black-wells by presenting myself in a shabby gown."

Hale rose, touched his cap in salute, and handed Blackwell her diploma.

Blushing furiously, she accepted it and started to leave the stage. But, her brother recalled, she suddenly turned back and said breathlessly, "Sir, I thank you. By the help of the Most High, it shall be the effort of my life to shed honor on this diploma." The church rang with applause as she and Hale bowed to each other. Then, Henry Blackwell later wrote his family, "our Sis, descending the steps, took her seat with her fellow physicians." Recalling the moment years later, Elizabeth Blackwell said she had felt "more thoroughly at home in the midst of these true-hearted young men than anywhere else in the town."

The commencement speaker, reported Henry Blackwell, "pronounced Elizabeth Blackwell the leader of her class; stated that she had passed a thorough course in every department, slighting none; that she had profited to the very utmost by all the advantages of the institution, and by her ladylike and dignified deportment had proved that the strongest intellect and nerve, the most untiring perseverance were compatible with the softest attributes of feminine delicacy and grace." All the students, he noted, showed their agreement by applauding wildly.

Now that Elizabeth Blackwell had been publicly honored, her former critics changed their attitude. After the ceremony, they flocked around the new doctor, and when she returned to her boardinghouse, many townswomen

called on her for the first time. Blackwell, who had spent two years in social isolation, was not impressed with her newfound admirers. "My room was thronged with visitors," she wrote in her diary. "I was glad of the sudden conversion thus shown, but my past experience had given me a useful and permanent lesson . . . as to the very shallow nature of popularity." Politely accepting congratulations, she packed her books and headed for Philadelphia, where she had begun her medical education several years earlier.

A woman earning a medical degree was news, and dozens of magazines

Henry Blackwell (above), Elizabeth's younger brother, attended her medical-school graduation. "Our sis," he told his family, "came off with flying colors."

Written in Latin, Elizabeth Blackwell's diploma was granted on January 23, 1849. It testified that she had completed 27 weeks of study at Geneva Medical College.

and newspapers reported the event. Most of the stories about Blackwell were friendly, but almost all were condescending. Although she had graduated at the head of her class, Boston's *Medical Journal* dismissed her as "a pretty little specimen of the feminine gender who walked into class with great composure." The British magazine *Punch* ran a humorous poem about "Doctrix Blackwell," suggesting that her medical training would add to her value as a wife. The Baltimore *Sun* congratulated her but recommended that she "confine her

practice . . . to diseases of the heart."

No one who knew Elizabeth Blackwell expected her to confine herself to anything. Her intelligence, fearlessness, and awesome energy had been apparent to her family from her earliest years. Born in Bristol, England, on February 3, 1821, Elizabeth was the third child of Hannah Lane Blackwell and her husband, Samuel, a prosperous sugar refiner. Preceding Elizabeth, whom her family called "Bessie," were her sisters Anna and Marian. After her came six more children: Samuel, Henry, Emily, Ellen, John, and George.

Hannah Lane and Samuel Blackwell had met at Bristol's Methodist church, where they both taught Sunday school. Intensely religious, the couple imbued their nine children with their own strong faith. Before breakfast every day, the family gathered to listen to Samuel Blackwell read from the Bible and pray. They attended morning and afternoon church services every Sunday and often went to prayer meetings during the week. At these sessions, recalled Elizabeth Blackwell in her autobiography, "Papa was sure to be called upon to pray, which he did very well." Bible reading and prayer also played a major role on social occasions; when the family had dinner guests, the evening usually ended with the entire company kneeling in worship.

Samuel Blackwell was sternly devoted to his religion, but he was also an affectionate and flexible parent. Once, for example, he discovered that his children were reading fiction, a practice his church considered sinful. Before punishing them, he agreed to read one of their books for himself. They gave him *Ivanhoe*, Sir Walter Scott's popular historical novel of 1819. He thought it was wonderful, and from that point on, fiction was permitted in the Blackwell household.

In her autobiography, Elizabeth Blackwell fondly recalled her father's "sense of fun, and his talent for rhyming." She wrote of the day that she, Anna, and Marian asked him if they

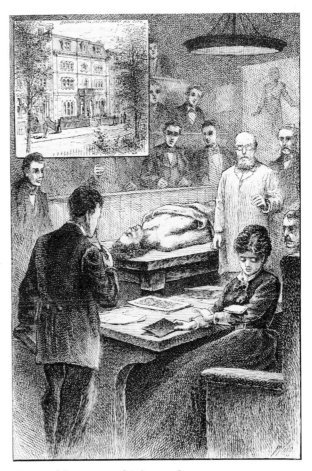

Tossed by a prankish student, a note lands on Blackwell's arm during an anatomy lecture. After she gained the respect of her classmates, such teasing stopped.

could share the family's large guest bed when their cousin came to visit. His reply came in the form of a humorous poem: "Such groaning! Such grunting!! Such sprawling about!!! / I could not allow such confusion and rout!!!!! / So this is my judgment—'tis wisdom you'll own, / *Two* beds for *four*

Mocking "Lady-Physicians," a 19th-century cartoon shows a young man "who has succeeded in catching a bad cold" in order to send for a pretty woman doctor.

girls are far better than one!" Another time, the girls asked if they could take their telescope to the roof of the family's house. "If I let you go there / I suppose your next prayer / Will be for a hop to the chimney top!" he responded, advising them to "keep on the earth, the place of your birth."

Less whimsical than her husband, Hannah Blackwell was equally enthusiastic about instilling spiritual values in her children. Gentle, soft spoken, and, according to one observer, "exquisitely pretty," she was assisted in her maternal chores by her four unmarried sisters-in-law. Of these women, the most formidable was Barbara Blackwell.

In her memoirs, Anna Blackwell described her "Aunt Bar" as "one of the most disagreeable, ill-tempered, strict, narrow-minded creatures alive; a dreadful tyrant, always quarreling with poor Mamma, who put up with insolence and spite that she ought not to have tolerated for an instant." Elizabeth Blackwell, less emotional than her sister, said only that Aunt Bar was the "somewhat stern though upright ruler of our youngest days."

All the Blackwell children shared memories of their aunt's "black book," a catalog of their juvenile sins. When a child had committed a certain number of offenses, Aunt Bar would send her or him to the attic without supper.

Still, the children were not physically disciplined. In an era when corporal punishment for childish offenses was common, the young Blackwells could count themselves fortunate in spite of their demanding aunt.

Another imposing family member was Samuel Blackwell, Sr., the children's grandfather. Loud voiced, hard drinking, hot tempered, and violently opinionated, Grandpapa Blackwell terrified everyone, especially his wife. Elizabeth Stokes Blackwell, for whom Elizabeth was named, often counseled her granddaughters about men. Anna Blackwell recalled her grandmother's advice in her memoirs. Young women, she said, should be suspicious of male flattery because "all *that* ceases when they'd got a woman to marry them, and then the poor girl found what a dreadful master marriage had given her." Grandmother Blackwell was evidently very convincing: Not one of her granddaughters ever married.

Although Samuel Blackwell had received no formal education, he was a tireless reader and had become, according to his daughter Anna, "an authority on almost any subject." He collected books, most of them religious or philosophical works, and he encouraged his children to read them. Most well-to-do British families of the time tutored their children at home. Sons were taught such subjects as Latin, mathematics, and astronomy; daughters learned French, music,

A deeply religious woman, Hannah Lane Blackwell (above) taught her children that spiritual health was just as important as physical well-being.

drawing, and embroidery. Samuel Blackwell, however, regarded his girls as "thinking creatures"; they studied the same subjects as their brothers.

Elizabeth, her father's favorite, inherited his independent spirit. In her autobiography, she wrote of spending cold winter nights on the nursery floor in the hope that she would strengthen her soul and harden her body against illness. She enjoyed testing her own endurance, at one point fasting for days in order to "subdue [her] physical nature." Such hardships, however, played little part in her childhood. She spent what she later called "very happy years" in a "comfortable family home, made by throwing two houses together, with its walled-in courtyard leading to the sugar refinery and my father's office."

The Blackwells' handsomely furnished house boasted a large upstairs playroom for the children and a huge drawing room, its fireplace flanked by twin pianos. Nevertheless, the Blackwell children spent most of their time outside, hiking and picnicking in the open fields that surrounded Bristol. Elizabeth would treasure memories of rambling though a landscape that included "breezy commons, lovely woods, clear streams, and waterfalls."

This tranquil existence was not to last. In 1832, when Elizabeth was 11 years old, her father announced that the family was moving to America. A number of factors had influenced Blackwell's decision. Following a period of prosperity in the 1820s, England had entered a period of economic depression. In 1831, widespread unemployment and political unrest had led to three days of furious rioting in Bristol, where angry mobs had burned public buildings, emptied local jails, and battled government troops.

Merchant ships enter Bristol's harbor. The British seaport, where Blackwell was born in 1821, was a thriving commercial and industrial center.

As friends wave farewell, emigrants leave England for the United States. The Blackwells traveled to New York on a similar vessel in 1832.

Hard on the heels of the riots came a collapse in sugar prices that almost wiped out Samuel Blackwell's business. Although a group of Bristol businessmen offered to lend him money, he detested the idea of being in debt and politely declined. It was time, he decided, to make a new start in a new country. In August 1832, the Blackwell family—father, pregnant mother, eight children, three aunts, a governess, and two servants—boarded the *Cosmo*, a small sailing ship bound for New York City.

Eleven years old when she arrived in the United States, Elizabeth Blackwell was legally a visitor for the next 17 years. She became an American citizen in 1849.

TWO

"Habits of Unconscious Independence"

The *Cosmo* took almost two months to cross the Atlantic Ocean. Most of the ship's 200 passengers spent their days in misery, violently ill from the constant pitching of the vessel and the cramped, airless cabins where they slept. Like her shipmates, 11-year-old Elizabeth Blackwell was seasick much of the time, but she enjoyed herself anyway. Sailing, she wrote later, furnished "delightful experiences to the younger travelers."

In October 1832, 53 days after they left Bristol, the emigrants beheld what Samuel Blackwell called a "truly thrilling" sight: the coast of America. Among the group, he noted in his journal, "scarcely a word was uttered—the fixed and eager eye and the gushing tear told their feelings better than

words." Standing on the deck of the *Cosmo*, Elizabeth gazed wide-eyed at her new home. In the 1830s, New York City's population was concentrated on the tip of the island; above that area were country homes and farms. The city, Elizabeth decided, looked like "a pleasant Dutch town, with comfortable houses standing in shady gardens."

When the Blackwells left the ship, they noticed that the city was oddly silent. Streets were almost deserted, windows were shuttered, shops were closed. New York, they soon learned, was in the grip of a cholera epidemic. Fearful of contracting the often deadly disease, many of the city's 200,000 residents had fled to the cleaner air of the suburbs. After moving into temporary quarters at a Manhattan hotel, the

British immigrants arrive in New York. The Blackwells' sailing ship took two months to cross the Atlantic; five years later, a steamship crossed in two weeks.

Blackwells knelt to give thanks for their safe journey and to pray for the victims of the epidemic.

A month after its arrival, the family settled into a house in the area now known as Greenwich Village. There, Hannah Blackwell gave birth to a son, named for the "father" of the family's new country. (Despite his distinguished name, George Washington Blackwell's parents and siblings called him "Washy.") By Christmas, the cholera epidemic was fading, and Samuel Blackwell was ready to start operating the sugar refinery he had established near the city's docks.

Skilled at his craft and familiar with the latest sugar-refining techniques, Blackwell encountered little difficulty in setting up his new business. What did give him trouble—as it had back in England—was the source of his sugar. The great sugar plantations of the Caribbean had always depended on slavery, an institution Blackwell detested. Because he was responsible for supporting a large family, he felt obliged to stick with the one trade he knew, but he had always been uneasy about it.

Hoping to disentangle the sugar business from slavery, Blackwell had experimented with manufacturing sugar from beets, but he had met with no success. Like their British counterparts, America's "sugar men" turned a deaf ear to the idea of developing a sugar-beet industry. But Blackwell was determined to do what he could to end slavery. His wife and children, who were equally opposed to the slave system, supported his efforts with enthusiasm.

The American abolition movement, which aimed at freeing all slaves, was supported by a small group of passionately committed believers, but theirs was not a popular cause. Shouting, jeering opponents often interrupted speeches by such prominent antislavery activists as William Lloyd Garrison and Theodore D. Weld, and the offices of abolitionist newspapers were periodically wrecked by angry mobs.

Undeterred by these violent displays, Samuel Blackwell aligned himself with the antislavery movement and

In this 1873 cartoon, "King Cholera" flees as New Yorkers scour the city. The connection between sanitation and health was little understood during the 1832 cholera epidemic.

A 19th-century sugar manufacturer inspects his refinery. Samuel Blackwell operated similar establishments in Bristol, New York City, and Cincinnati.

its leaders. He introduced himself to Garrison by leaping onto the platform after one of the abolitionist's impassioned speeches, shaking his hand vigorously, and expressing his own heartfelt opposition to slavery. Garrison was impressed. By the fall of 1833, he was a frequent visitor at the Blackwell home, where his fiery conversation and gift for storytelling made him popular with the children.

Everyone in the Blackwell family made baskets, cakes, and toys to be sold at the huge 1834 Anti-Slavery Fair, held in New York to raise funds for the movement. Soon after this event, Elizabeth and her family played a small but exciting role in the abolitionist drama.

It began when a clergyman friend, the Reverend Samuel Cox, gave an antislavery sermon in which he remarked that Christ was not a member of the Caucasian race. Accusing Cox of "calling Jesus a nigger," a furious mob descended on his home, threatening to hang him from the nearest tree.

Cox, who had been warned of the mob's intentions, piled his family into a carriage and raced to the Blackwell home. They were welcomed with open arms. Immediately offering their own rooms to the minister's five children, Elizabeth and her sisters moved into the attic. It was cramped and stiflingly hot, but for two weeks—until it was safe for the Coxes to return to their

Slaves chop cane on a Caribbean sugar plantation. Although his livelihood depended on such sugar, Samuel Blackwell detested slavery.

Fiery abolitionist William Lloyd Garrison (above), founder of the American Anti-Slavery Society, established a firm friendship with Samuel Blackwell and his family.

home—the girls cheerfully slept on the attic floor, proud that they could help people who stood up for their convictions.

By 1835 the Blackwells had outgrown their narrow townhouse, and Hannah and Samuel decided to move their 11-member family across the Hudson River to Jersey City. The youngsters were delighted with their new home, a large house overlooking the river and, beyond it, New York City. Surrounding the residence were fields and woods, ideal territory for games among the close-knit Blackwells.

Because there were no schools in Jersey City, then a small farming community, the older children commuted to New York. Like their father, who crossed the river each day to get to his office, they made the trip by ferry. Elizabeth Blackwell, now 14 years old, enjoyed her new life-style, which created, she noted in her autobiography, "habits of unconscious independence." If an abolition meeting or concert kept her or her sisters out late, she added, "the hourly ferryboat would be missed, and we have crossed by the 11 or 12 o'clock boat, with no risk or experience of annoyance."

With Elizabeth's newfound feeling of independence came awareness of what she called "the restrictions which confine my dear sex." Career choices available to women of her time were extremely limited. The only self-supporting women she knew were her Aunts Barbara and Lucy, who had opened a hat store in Manhattan. But the life of a milliner held no appeal for Elizabeth. "I wish I could devise some good way of maintaining myself," she wrote in her diary.

Meanwhile, she was determined to educate herself, often working far into the night on her school assignments. She was a good student in most subjects, particularly history and philosophy, but she thoroughly disliked her class in physiology, the study of living organisms and their functions. In *Lone Woman*, Blackwell biographer Dorothy Clarke Wilson writes of the day when Elizabeth's physiology teacher, eager to demonstrate the complex mechanisms of sight, brought the eye of a bull to class. "Elizabeth took one horrified glance" at the eye "and fled precipitately to the restroom," reports Wilson.

In her diary, Elizabeth criticized herself for showing such "physical weakness," resolving to improve. Soon afterward, she suffered an attack of "intermittent fever," a form of malaria that produces alternating bouts of severe chills and high temperatures. Refusing to give in to the ailment, the young woman tried, she later recalled, "to walk it off" by taking a hike in the country, then shutting herself in a dark closet. By the time her Aunt Bar discovered her, she was dehydrated and delirious. Stern as always, Barbara Blackwell told her niece she was "acting the fool," and that it was a sign of "vanity" to refuse to admit to illness.

Elizabeth listened to her aunt, but she would never abandon her efforts to master what she regarded as her weaknesses. In fact, however, she was unusually strong, especially for a girl of her size. Shorter and more slender than her sturdy siblings, she was agile, energetic, and seemingly tireless. She could outrun and outclimb brothers as well as sisters, and her graceful, long-fingered hands were extraordinarily powerful. Still, with her shy disposition and pale skin, eyes, and hair, she saw herself as a dim shadow of her vivacious, attractive sisters. "Afraid I shall never learn to dance gracefully," reads a typical diary entry from her teenage years. Another day, she wrote, "I think sometimes a hermit's life would suit me very well."

Despite such self-criticism, Elizabeth enjoyed life in New Jersey. In the winters, she joined her brothers and sisters in ice skating and sleigh riding; in the summers, they fished, rode horses, and took long walks. Elizabeth particularly enjoyed tramping through the surrounding fields and forests with Samuel, Jr., whom she called her "companion brother." The two spent much of their time together talking about books they had read and discussing the possibilities of the future.

This pleasant existence was not to last. New York City, its buildings largely constructed of wood, was the scene of frequent fires. In 1836, when Elizabeth was 15, Samuel Blackwell's sugar refinery burned to the ground. Because the city's insurance companies had been bankrupted by a gigantic fire the year before, Blackwell received no compensation for his loss. Although he had acquired a part interest in a second refinery, his income was sharply decreased, and his family was obliged to revise its habits.

Hannah Blackwell dismissed her

The Great Fire of 1835, one of the worst in Manhattan's history, consumes an entire city block. Samuel Blackwell's sugar refinery burned the following year.

servants, dividing the household chores among her daughters. Elizabeth responded to her new assignment much as any teenager might. "This is my day for seeing to the meals," she wrote in her diary one morning. "I hate the employment and look with real dread to my week, for we have agreed to take it by weeks. I fear we shall not have much pleasure in life now." Another entry reads, "Papa gave Mamma a little money and told her it must last the week. We all had to go to bed in the dark."

Elizabeth, who had been practicing on the piano for five hours a day, was distressed when she had to give up her music lessons. Her father's birthday brought more gloom: "We did not give him any present, our purses being so low," she wrote sadly. She and her siblings worried about their once-high-spirited father, who had almost stopped talking to his family and whose mood seemed darker with every passing day. "What his plans are for the future," wrote Elizabeth in her diary, "we do not know. I suppose it will be something about beets!" She was right.

Samuel Blackwell had been reading books on sugar-beet production and

German workers process sugar beets. Disturbed by the use of slave-produced cane sugar, Samuel Blackwell tried to develop such factories in the United States.

experimenting with beet-sugar formulas on the kitchen stove. In 1837, a cousin who had moved to Cincinnati, Ohio, came to visit. Claiming that this "Athens of the West" offered unlimited opportunity and a perfect climate for raising beets, and noting that there were no sugar refineries in the area, the cousin urged Blackwell to investigate for himself. Intrigued, he went to Cincinnati in early 1838. He returned full of enthusiasm for the frontier town. The family, he announced, would move there as quickly as possible.

A trio of sidewheelers, smoke billowing from their tall stacks, cruise Cincinnati's bustling harbor. The Blackwells moved to the Ohio River city in 1838.

THREE

"A Separate Existence"

In the spring of 1838, the Blackwells packed their books and china, sold their furniture, and put their Jersey City house up for rent. Heading for Ohio were seven Blackwell children, their parents, and their Aunt Mary. Elizabeth's sisters Anna and Marian had taken teaching jobs and remained in the East. Aunt Bar (who would die of cholera a few months afterward) moved in with Anna, and Aunt Lucy married and returned to England. "We left New York full of hope and eager anticipation," wrote Elizabeth Blackwell in her autobiography.

The 656-mile journey from New York to Cincinnati took 9 days. The Blackwells traveled to Philadelphia by ship, then boarded one of the "large and splendid eight-wheel cars" of the Pioneer Fast Line. Elizabeth later recalled that she and her family "were de-

lighted with the magnificent scenery of the mountains and rivers as we crossed Pennsylvania." After traversing the Allegheny Mountains on the horse-powered Portage Railroad and making their way up the Ohio River on a side-wheel steamboat, the Blackwells finally reached their destination.

Cincinnati was a pleasant surprise. Half expecting to find a raw frontier town, the family discovered a busy and prosperous little city with neat brick houses, leafy chestnut trees, and well-dressed, friendly citizens. Samuel Blackwell leased a large stone home for his family and a mill where he could open a sugar refinery. Elizabeth began tutoring her younger siblings and teaching piano to neighboring children. The Blackwells eagerly explored their new surroundings, taking part in such unfamiliar activities as

Outspoken British author Harriet Martineau (above) offended many straitlaced Americans with her radical views about feminism, religion, and abolition.

public Fourth of July picnics and huge outdoor religious rallies. "For a few months," wrote Elizabeth Blackwell in her autobiography, "we enjoyed the strange incidents of early western civilization, so different from the older society of the East."

After those first few months, however, a dark shadow fell across the Blackwell household. Despite his renewed optimism about the future, Samuel Blackwell was obviously unwell, increasingly silent and exhausted. In July he began to run high temperatures and suffer from bouts of fainting. Diagnosed as "bilious fever," his illness

was probably a recurrence of malaria, which he had contracted earlier. By August it was clear that his days were numbered.

Aware of his impending death, Blackwell asked his wife to sit close to him on his bed. Elizabeth's brother Samuel recorded his words. "Dear love," he said, "manage your own affairs. There is the house and furniture and nothing to pay till the end of the year. . . . But I am sorry to say that I have no money to leave you." The next day, as Elizabeth held his hand in her own, Samuel Blackwell died at the age of 48.

"I felt as if all hope and joy were gone," wrote the grieving Elizabeth after her father's funeral. "I hated the light and the beautiful day and the people who stared at us. I seemed alone in the world." When the Blackwells took stock of their affairs, they discovered they had $20 in cash, a partially furnished house, and a stack of medical and funeral bills. At this point, they also learned that the agent who had sold their furniture in New Jersey had disappeared with the money. Life, however, had to go on.

The next day Elizabeth recommenced her music teaching. Her 14-year-old brother, Sam, got a job as an office clerk, and 13-year-old Henry hired himself out as an errand boy. "We entered upon the sternest realities of life—a struggle for existence without connections, without experience," recalled Elizabeth later. A month after their father's death, Anna and Marian joined their family in Cincinnati.

The three oldest Blackwell daughters, along with their Aunt Mary, decided to open a boarding school, to be called the Cincinnati English and French Academy for Young Ladies. Somewhat to their surprise, the handbills they printed to advertise the school brought in a dozen students as well as much-needed income. (Each pupil paid $100 per year for tuition and board.)

Just as the school was getting under way, the family experienced another painful loss. Aunt Mary, 48 years old, was suddenly stricken with the same ailment that had killed her brother two months earlier. Within a few days she, too, was dead. "Now it seemed as if whatever arrived, I should never feel again," wrote the sorrowful Elizabeth in her diary. But with the aid of their mother, who took charge of the kitchen, the three sisters managed to carry on. They worked long hours, teaching such subjects as arithmetic, grammar, history, botany, and philosophy.

The economic independence Elizabeth had longed for was now a brutal necessity. "For the next few years, until the younger children grew up and were able gradually to share in the work, we managed to support the family and maintain a home," she recalled later. Only 17 years old, she had little

William Blackstone (above) codified British and American common law. Legally, said the 18th-century British jurist, women had no "separate existence."

confidence in her abilities as a teacher. "I was afraid of my pupils," she wrote in her diary. "The elder girls were very wild western young women, utterly unaccustomed to discipline. I only controlled them by a steady quietness . . . which they took for sternness, but which was really fear."

She continued her teaching, but she never learned to like it. "By the time school was over, I was almost distracted," she wrote one day. "I really think if anyone came and offered [proposed] to me, I should have accepted without hesitation." Soon after remarking that she would accept "anyone,"

An auctioneer takes bids on a black couple and their baby. Blackwell said living in the slaveholding state of Kentucky gave her "an intense longing to scream."

Blackwell agreed to go for a drive with a would-be suitor she had met in church. Her mild interest in him, however, ended after a few hours of conversation.

The suitor, she noted with disdain, had not only "associated with low people," he had "nothing like refinement or literary taste, and betrayed his commonness of mind." A few weeks later, she attended a lecture on current events. "Came home followed by some young man," she recalled tersely, "but as I thought I could knock him down if necessary, I did not much mind."

Blackwell's confidence in her own strength was not exaggerated. Her brother Samuel recalled one evening when Thomas Emery, a family friend, came to visit. During the evening, Emery happened to remark that not even the strongest female had the physical power of the weakest male. Samuel disagreed, telling Emery that "our Elib here" was "more than a match" for himself or his brother Henry. "She can even carry us around," he said. When Emery laughed at such an absurd statement, the diminutive Elizabeth picked him up and, ignoring his struggles, marched him across the parlor. Her brothers roared, but Elizabeth just smiled. Later that night, she recorded the event in her diary. With quiet triumph she wrote, "I carried Mr. E. around the room."

This incident reflected Blackwell's increasing impatience with the position of women in her society. Her attitude was similar to that of Harriet Martineau, a British writer who visited the United States in 1837. "While women's intellect is confined, her morals crushed, her health ruined, her weakness encouraged, and her strength punished, she is told that her lot is cast in the paradise of women," said Martineau. "And there is no country in the world where there is so much boasting of the 'chivalrous' treatment she enjoys. In short, indulgence is given her as a substitute for justice, and marriage is the only object left open to women."

After listening to a sermon one Sunday, Blackwell wrote that the clergyman "gave some rather unjust and quite uncalled for remarks on the inferiority of women." And when she had finished a popular novel called *Romance and Reality*, she wrote, "I do not like many of the sentiments at all and think the author is exceedingly unjust to the ladies."

At this point in American history, a married woman's rights were practically nonexistent. Everything she had owned before her marriage became her husband's property. After marrying, she could not sue or be sued in a court of law, appear as a witness, make a will, or even claim her own children.

Following English common law, American law held that "a man cannot grant anything to his wife ... for to grant would be to suppose her separate existence."

A separate existence, however, was exactly what Elizabeth Blackwell yearned for. With her sisters she continued to support the family for several years, but by 1842 Henry and Sam were old enough to earn men's salaries— much higher, of course, than women's. The two young men were soon making more money than their three sisters

Clergyman Lyman Beecher (above) was known for thrift as well as piety. Seeing a new rug in his parlor, a neighbor once exclaimed, "All this and heaven too, Lyman!"

37

combined, and the women decided to close their school. Anna Blackwell left to teach at a school in New York State, and when Elizabeth received an invitation to take charge of a school in Kentucky, she jumped at the chance.

Her family was doubtful about her moving to a slave state that was, said Sam Blackwell, "beyond the verge of

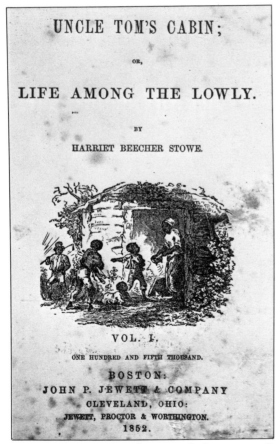

UNCLE TOM'S CABIN;

OR,

LIFE AMONG THE LOWLY.

BY

HARRIET BEECHER STOWE.

VOL. I.

ONE HUNDRED AND FIFTH THOUSAND.

BOSTON:
JOHN P. JEWETT & COMPANY
CLEVELAND, OHIO:
JEWETT, PROCTOR & WORTHINGTON.
1852.

Uncle Tom's Cabin hastened the start of America's bloody civil conflict. Meeting author Stowe, Abraham Lincoln reportedly remarked, "So this is the little lady who made this great war."

civilization," but she was determined to make the move. Her only alternatives seemed to be marriage or a life as a "maiden aunt," teaching music and living at home as her own aunts had done. Neither prospect appealed to her. In March 1844 she boarded a steamboat and headed down the Ohio River. She was disheartened by her first view of her new home, Henderson, Kentucky. She described it to her family as "a dirty, little, straggling, country village" whose residents were "in the lowest degree uninteresting, with nothing to do but knit, nothing to hear but their own petty affairs."

After she started teaching, Blackwell's attitude toward her neighbors softened. "My school," she wrote her family, "is limited to 21; it has been full for some time, and many have been refused. The girls are a good, pleasant set, much more gentle than in Cincinnati." Henderson's citizens, she added, "begin to interest me more than they did at first; all continue very kind." She had, she added, been "amused to learn accidentally how I have been talked over in every direction, and my teeth particularly admired in peculiarly Kentucky style. 'Well, I do declare she's got a clean mouth, hasn't she?'—white teeth seeming remarkable where all use tobacco!"

Blackwell said she thought the townspeople were "a little afraid of me, particularly when they see me read German." The town's young male pop-

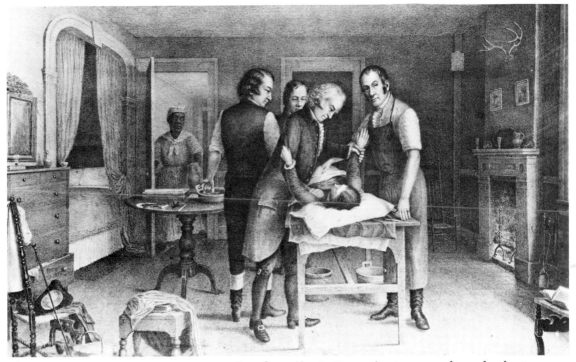

Physicians prepare to operate on a female patient. Too prim to consult male doctors about gynecological problems, many Victorian women suffered needlessly.

ulation, however, seemed to find her more attractive than frightening. Before long, she told her family, she had acquired two admirers, "one tall, the other short, with very pretty names, of good family and with tolerable fortune, but unfortunately one seems to me a dolt, the other, well, not wise, so I keep them at a respectful distance, which you know I am quite capable of doing."

Blackwell might have learned to enjoy her job in Henderson, but she could not come to terms with life in a slave society. Thinking about it, she told her family, gave her "an intense longing to scream." She said she could not bear to be "in the midst of beings degraded to the utmost in body and mind, drudging on from earliest morning to latest night, cuffed about by everyone, scolded at all day long, blamed unjustly, and without spirit enough to reply, with no consideration in any way for their feelings, with no hope of the future.... To live in their midst, utterly unable to help them, is to me dreadful, and what I would not do long for any consideration."

Blackwell meant what she said. She resigned after one term, going back to Cincinnati in the late summer of 1844. "The family life was full and active," she recalled in her autobiography, "and for a while I keenly enjoyed the return home." She also enjoyed meeting her family's new friends, who in-

A young woman comforts an ailing friend. Blackwell's dying neighbor, Mary Donaldson, said that a woman doctor would have made her illness easier to bear.

cluded the celebrated Presbyterian clergyman Lyman Beecher and his daughter, Harriet Beecher Stowe.

Blackwell attended Anti-Slavery Society meetings, listened to lectures on abolition, went for long walks with her brothers, and joined a group of women who made clothing for escaped slaves. At the invitation of Harriet Stowe, she joined the Semi-Colon Club, a literary association whose membership included many of Cincinnati's leading writers, professors, lawyers, and scientists.

Stowe—who would publish the immensely popular antislavery novel *Uncle Tom's Cabin* in 1851—was the group's star, often reading aloud from her stories and essays. Impressed with the 24-year-old Blackwell's crisply stated opinions, Stowe, 34, told a friend, "She has tact and quickness of perception that I trust." Blackwell returned Stowe's admiration, and the two became good friends.

Nevertheless, Blackwell was restless. Before long, she later recalled, she "felt the want of a more engrossing pursuit than the study of music, German, and metaphysics, and the ordinary interests that social life presented." At this point, she visited a sick friend, a simple act that would have immensely important consequences.

The friend, a neighbor named Mary Donaldson, was dying of cancer. After chatting with her for a few minutes, Blackwell rose to leave, but Donaldson stopped her. Blackwell described the scene in her autobiography. "You are fond of study, have health and leisure," said Donaldson. "Why not study medicine?"

Blackwell was stunned by the question. She told Donaldson her suggestion was "impossible," that she "hated everything connected with the body and could not bear the sight of a medical book." She recalled the time she had "tried to walk off the deadly chill" of malaria, her attempts to strengthen her body by sleeping on the cold floor and going without food, and her revulsion at the sight of the bull's eye her teacher had brought to class. "The very thought of dwelling on the physical structure of the body and its various ailments filled me with disgust," she said later. Anyway, she reminded Donaldson, there was no such thing as a woman doctor. The whole idea was absurd.

"If I could have been treated by a lady doctor," said Donaldson gently, "my worst sufferings would have been spared me." Blackwell knew this was true. Along with the physical pain of what was probably uterine cancer, Donaldson had been exposed to the emotional agony and embarrassment of being examined and treated by a male doctor. Blackwell was aware that "the delicate nature" of her friend's affliction had "made the methods of treatment a constant suffering for her." Discussing gynecological problems with a man was torture to any Victorian woman raised to value modesty. Had Donaldson been able to consult a woman doctor, she might have reported her symptoms earlier and, with an earlier diagnosis, have had a chance of recovery.

Quite clearly, the medical profession needed women in its ranks. Gynecological problems, increased by poor diet, confining clothes, lack of exercise, repeated childbearing, and ignorance about hygiene, were widespread. In her book *Significant Sisters: The Grassroots of Feminism* Margaret Forster notes that the most common female affliction of the mid-19th century, vaginal infections known as "uterine

A Victorian woman demurely allows a suitor to take her hand. When Blackwell realized that the man she loved expected her to be equally "ladylike," she rejected him.

catarrh," kept "a quarter of the female population in bed for half their lives."

Blackwell, as she noted in her diary, was "shocked by Miss Donaldson's prayer that I should become a physician," but it had impressed her deeply. "I resolutely tried for weeks to put the ideas suggested by my friend away," she recalled later, "but it constantly recurred to me." She had something else on her mind as well: a member of what she called "the other sex."

Blackwell had no desire to form a "life association"—marriage—with any man, knowing she would be bound to obey and serve him forever. She was, however, strongly attracted to men. "I

Harriet Beecher Stowe (above) was a staunch abolitionist but a lukewarm feminist. She called Blackwell's dream of becoming a doctor "impracticable."

never remember the time," she wrote a year later, "when I had not suffered more or less from the common malady—falling in love." At Harriet Stowe's literary club, she had met a cultured and handsome man who showed a marked interest in her. He called for her, walked her home from lectures and meetings, and brought her flowers, a clear statement of affection in Victorian days.

Delighted with the man's company (she never mentioned his name, even in her diary), Blackwell lent him some of her favorite books on philosophy. His response put an end to her thoughts of a "close and ennobling companionship." Such books, he told her, were better suited to masculine

minds; a woman should content herself with poetry and essays.

Much as she admired him, Blackwell could not bear the thought of being dependent on someone who did not respect her intelligence. She was a strong-willed, capable woman, and she wanted to earn her own way and speak her own mind. She had saved the flowers her suitor had brought her; now she sadly put them away in a package. She labeled it "young love's last dream."

At this point she was determined, she wrote in her diary, to "place a strong barrier between me and all ordinary marriage." She said she needed "something to engross my thoughts, some object in life which will fill this vacuum and prevent this sad wearing away of the heart." Slowly it dawned on her that Donaldson's suggestion might be that "something." And becoming a doctor might answer her undefined longing to engage in important work.

Women, Blackwell believed, had special qualities, including maternal instincts, that could make them valuable to the field of medicine. Breaking the age-old taboo against women doctors would call for sacrifice, determination, and courage. But what better way to spend one's life than fighting a great moral battle, one that would be waged not only for oneself, but for other women, both living and yet to be born? Finally, Blackwell wrote in her diary, "I made up my mind to devote myself to medical study."

Deeply religious like the rest of her family, Blackwell prayed over her decision. "I thought much on my future course, and turned for aid to that Friend with whom I am beginning to hold true communion," she recalled later. "Jesus Christ must be a living spirit, and have the power of communicating with us, for one thought towards Him dispels all evil, and . . . produces peace unspeakable."

Family members, wrote Blackwell, "showed the warmest sympathy" with her plans, but her friend Harriet Beecher Stowe was less supportive. Stowe told Blackwell it would be "impracticable" for her to become a doctor. Such a project, she said, would run into strong prejudice and crushing opposition. She finally conceded that if such a thing were possible, it might be "highly useful" to have a woman doctor, but Blackwell could extract no further encouragement from her.

After consulting with Stowe, Blackwell approached a prominent Cincinnati doctor who was familiar with the medical schools of Paris. When she asked him about her chances of studying there, he was "horrified," she recalled. "The method of instruction was such," he said, "that no American or English lady could stay there three weeks." Most of the other friends Blackwell consulted were equally negative, but one of them, a fellow literary-

Using a cadaver as a prop, an anatomy professor lectures medical students. Until Blackwell decided to become a doctor, such audiences never included women.

club member named James Perkins, was different. He said, "I do wish you would take the matter up, if you have the courage—and you have courage, I know."

Perkins's optimism, said Blackwell, made her feel as though she "could conquer the world." She decided that she had the intelligence, the strength, and the moral courage to be a pioneer. She would show the world that it was not "impracticable" for a woman to study and practice medicine, and she would prove that women could improve the field of medicine in the bargain. Mary Donaldson died a few weeks after her conversation with Blackwell, but her death marked the birth of a new day in medical history.

Advised that attending medical school was "impossible," Blackwell was undismayed. "This verdict," she said later, "was rather an encouragement than otherwise."

FOUR

"Trust in God and Mock at the Devil!"

By 1845 the Blackwells were solvent, but far from rich. A medical education—then as now—meant a huge outlay of cash, far more than Elizabeth Blackwell's family could ever supply. "Thrown thus entirely on my own resources," she wrote in her autobiography, "I finally resolved to accept a teacher's position in a school in North Carolina, where, while accumulating money for future use, I could also commence a trial of medical study." The school's principal, John Dickson, was a former doctor. He had an outstanding medical library to which he promised Blackwell full access.

"With loving goodbyes and some tears," wrote Blackwell, "I left home for Asheville, North Carolina, to begin preparations for my unknown career."

Accompanied by 2 of her brothers in a horse-drawn carriage, she traveled through Kentucky and Tennessee and across the Allegheny Mountains in 11 days. The night before her brothers returned to Ohio, she had an emotional experience she would never forget. She described the moment in her autobiography.

"I retired to my bedroom and gazed from the open window long and mournfully at the dim mountain outlines visible in the starlight—mountains which seemed to shut me away hopelessly from all I cared for. . . . I was overwhelmed with sudden terror of what I was undertaking. In an agony of mental despair I cried out, 'Oh God, help me! Support me! Lord Jesus, guide, enlighten me!' My very being went out in this cry for Divine help. Suddenly, overwhelmingly, an answer came. A glorious presence, as of brilliant light, flooded my soul.... All doubt as to the future, all hesitation as to the rightfulness of my purpose, left me, and never in afterlife returned. I *knew* that, however insignificant my individual effort might be, it was in a right direction."

While she was in Asheville, Blackwell boarded at the home of the school principal and his wife. She taught music during the day and read medical books at night. It was in Asheville that she performed her first dissection. The subject of her operation was a dead beetle, laughingly presented to "the future doctress" by a fellow teacher.

Blackwell was determined to be a doctor, but she had not yet gotten over her squeamishness. Nevertheless, she held the insect down with a hairpin and prepared to cut it open with her penknife. "The effort to do this," she recalled later, "was so repugnant that it was some time before I could compel myself to make the necessary incision." After she finally performed the "operation," she was pleased with herself. Never again, she said in her autobiography, was she seriously bothered by anatomical studies.

Blackwell liked Asheville and its residents, and she was pleased to be both earning money and learning about medicine from Dickson's books. Still, North Carolina was a slave state. Blackwell realized she could do little to ease the lot of the slaves, but remaining silent deeply disturbed her conscience. She told her mother that she

The Alleghenies tower above Asheville, North Carolina, pictured here in the 1840s. Blackwell said the sight of these mountains renewed her strength.

Former slaves learn to read and write in a post–Civil War classroom. When Blackwell tried to start a similar school in 1845, she learned her plan was illegal.

sometimes hated herself for "the calmness with which I answer some outrageous injustice, when I am really raging with indignation." However, she said, "the slightest display of feeling arms all their prejudices, and I am no orator to convert by a burst of passionate eloquence."

Instead of trying to convert anyone, she decided to open a school for slave children. Then she learned that North Carolina law prohibited anyone from teaching a black person to read and write. Calling this state of affairs "intolerable," Blackwell next proposed a Sunday school, where slave children could at least be taught Bible stories. This effort was more successful, but

even so, Blackwell told her mother, it seemed wrong to teach these "degraded little beings" a religion that their "owners profess to follow while violating its very first principles." But she contined to teach, deciding that her best course was simply "to go on in my own quiet manner, knowing that it does not proceed from cowardice."

In 1846 Dickson announced that he was closing his school. He suggested that Blackwell, whom he had come to admire, move to Charleston, South Carolina. There she could get a teaching job and board with his brother's family. Blackwell was pleased: Samuel H. Dickson was both a respected practicing physician and a professor at

Charleston's medical college. She could add to her tuition funds while continuing her medical education.

Like his brother, Sam Dickson was impressed with Blackwell and her determination to become a doctor. He started instructing her in Greek, organized a study program for her in his extensive medical library, and got her a job teaching music. "Every morning a couple of hours were devoted before breakfast to learning the necessary rudiments of Greek," Blackwell recalled. After that came eight hours of teaching piano, then a long evening with Dickson's medical books. In her rare moments of free time, Blackwell earned extra money by translating German fiction into English.

A runaway slave is recaptured by his master. Although Blackwell respected many southerners, she could not adjust to a society that kept humans in bondage.

During the year she spent in Charleston, Blackwell wrote to many of the nation's leading physicians and sent application letters to all the major medical schools. Few of the doctors bothered to respond to her inquiries, and from the schools came nothing but silence. At last, however, she received a friendly letter from Joseph Warrington, a prominent Philadelphia doctor. Warrington told Blackwell she would be wiser to pursue a career as a nurse than as a doctor. After all, he pointed out, woman was designed to be man's helpmate, not his equal. But he did add one encouraging note: If her "project be of divine origin and appointment," he said, "it will sooner or later surely be accomplished."

In May 1847 Blackwell decided it was time to storm the citadel: Philadelphia, the medical capital of the country. Dr. Dickson gave her several letters of introduction to colleagues in the Pennsylvania city. Armed with the letters and her "carefully hoarded earnings," she bought passage on a merchant ship and headed north. In Philadelphia she paid a call on Dr. William Elder, a friend of Dickson's. Elder and his wife invited her to stay with them, and she accepted gratefully.

Next, Blackwell applied to Philadelphia's four large medical schools. While she waited to hear from them, she arranged to take private anatomy lessons from a local specialist. To avoid

Blackwell spent a year studying medicine in Charleston, South Carolina, seen here in an 1840 engraving. She described the South as "strange and beautiful."

embarrassing his female pupil, the anatomy tutor tactfully started out with a lesson on the human wrist. "The beauty of the tendons and exquisite arrangements of this part of the body struck my artistic sense," Blackwell wrote later.

Her medical-school interviews were, she noted wryly, "often amusing." "Well, what is it? What do you want?" barked the first school administrator she met. When she told him she wanted to study medicine, he roared with laughter. Calming down, he said he would look into the matter and let her know. His final answer, however, was no: The school's entire staff opposed admitting a woman. Perhaps, he said, she would have better luck applying to medical school in New England.

The doctor who interviewed her at the next school was worse: He simply sat and stared at her in silence. After she "harangued him," as she put it in her diary, he said, "I cannot express my opinion to you either one way or another." Blackwell pleaded for some advice, but the doctor said he was "not at liberty to unfold the operation of [his] mind." Finally, she wrote, "I got up in despair, leaving his mind to take action on the subject at his leisure."

"You cannot expect us to furnish you with a stick to break our heads with," said the dean of another medical school. Blackwell was astonished: The male medical establishment was actually worried about competition, concerned about "the rapid practical success which would attend a lady doctor!" Meeting nothing but negative responses from Philadelphia schools, Blackwell asked her friend Dr. Warrington to confer with one of his Paris-trained colleagues about the possibility of studying in the French capital.

The colleague refused even to meet Blackwell, advising Warrington that she should abandon her desire for a medical education. No American medical school would accept her, and a French school would be "a horrible place" for a "young, unmarried lady."

Charleston physician Samuel H. Dickson (above) encouraged Blackwell's medical ambitions. He also gave her a room, found her a job, and taught her Greek.

She told Warrington, she wrote in her diary, "that if the path of duty led me to hell I would go there; and I did not think that by being with devils I should become a devil myself—at which the good doctor stared."

Despite her brave words, Blackwell did not want to go to another country to study. Nor did she want to attend medical school dressed as a man, a recommendation made by several well-meaning acquaintances. "Neither the advice to go to Paris nor the suggestion of a disguise tempted me for a moment," she remarked in her autobiography. "It was to my mind a moral crusade on which I had entered, a course of justice and common sense, and it must be pursued in the light of day, and with public sanction, in order to accomplish its end."

Realizing that prospects were nonexistent in Philadelphia, Blackwell went to New York City in July 1847. Here, too, the doors of the medical schools were firmly closed against her, but she returned to Philadelphia with a list of smaller schools in the Northeast. She applied to 12—making a total of 29 she had written to—and once again sat down to wait for replies. One after another, the responses arrived; one after another, they turned her down as an "inappropriate" candidate. Then, in late October, she opened a letter from Geneva College in upstate New York. She could hardly believe what she read.

A 1910 photograph of Hobart (formerly Geneva) College shows Blackwell House (right), a women's dormitory named for the school's first female graduate.

First was a note from Charles Lee, dean of the Geneva faculty. Blackwell's unusual application, he said, had been submitted to the student body, whose members had acted "entirely on their own behalf, without any interference on the part of the faculty." Enclosed, noted Lee, was the result of the students' deliberations.

"The entire medical class of Geneva College," said the student declaration, has "resolved that one of the radical principles of a republican government is the universal education of both sexes; that to every branch of scientific education the door should be equally open to all; that the application of Elizabeth Blackwell to become a member of our class meets our entire approbation [approval]."

Lee told Blackwell he was sure she could, "by judicious management, not only 'disarm criticism,' but elevate yourself without detracting in the least from the dignity of the profession." He wished her success in her undertaking, which, he said, "some may deem bold in the present state of society."

"With an immense sigh of relief and . . . profound gratitude to Providence," recalled Blackwell later, "I instantly accepted the invitation and prepared for the journey to western New York State." Her delight might have been tempered if she had known what happened at Geneva before the invitation

51

Blackwell's college classmate Stephen Smith (above) became one of her greatest admirers. He said it would be "impossible to magnify the power of [her] personality."

class. For a minute or two . . . there was a pause, then the ludicrousness of the situation seemed to seize the entire class, and a perfect Babel of talk, laughter, and catcalls followed. Congratulations upon the new source of excitement were everywhere heard. . . . At length the question was put to a vote, and the whole class arose and voted 'Aye.' "

The students had voted to accept Blackwell as a joke, but because the Geneva faculty had left the decision up to them, the matter was settled: For the first time, a woman would attend an American medical school. Blackwell arrived in Geneva on the night of November 6. The next day she was registered as student number 130 and escorted to her first class by Dean Lee. Once more, Stephen Smith reported on the event:

"A hush fell over the class as if each member had been stricken by paralysis," he recalled. "A death-like stillness prevailed during the lecture, and only the newly arrived student took notes. . . . It is quite impossible to magnify the power of the personality of Miss Blackwell over the lawless elements of that class. . . . The moment that she entered upon the platform the most perfect order and quiet prevailed."

Blackwell rented a room in a nearby boardinghouse and settled into her new life. At first she was disturbed by the inquisitive, sometimes hostile glances she attracted. "The ladies

was sent out. Dr. Warrington had sent a letter recommending her as "a lady medical student." The Geneva administrators were opposed to admitting a woman, but they did not want to offend the distinguished Warrington. Their solution was to leave the decision to the students, who, they believed, would be sure to vote against admitting her. But the students had surprised them.

Many years later, one of those students, Dr. Stephen Smith, described the meeting where Blackwell's future was decided. "The faculty did not understand the tone and temper of the stopped to stare at me," she recalled, "as at a curious animal." She decided to ignore them and concentrate on her fellow students. With them, she said, she "soon felt perfectly at home." Soon after she began classes, Dean Lee introduced her to anatomy professor James Webster, who would become her good friend.

Webster, described by Blackwell as "a little plump man, blunt in manner and very voluble [talkative]," shook her hand, congratulated her for being there, and asked what branches of medicine she had studied. "I told him all but surgery," she reported in a letter to her family.

"Well," said Dr. Lee, "do you mean to practice surgery?"

"Why, of course she does," broke in Dr. Webster. "Only think what a well-educated woman would do in a city like New York. Why, my dear sir, she'd have her hands full in no time; her success would be immense. Yes, yes, you'll go through the course, and get your diploma with great *éclat* [style] too; we'll give you the opportunities. You'll make a stir, I can tell you."

Blackwell's fellow students were friendly, but when she was present during lectures on "delicate" subjects, they found it hard to remain serious. Even she had to fight to keep from giggling. In her diary, she described an anatomy class whose subject was the human reproductive organs. "That dissection was just as much as I could

bear. Some of the students blushed, some were hysterical, not one could keep in a smile. . . . I had to pinch my hand till the blood nearly came, and call on Christ to help me from smiling, for that would have ruined everything."

During her early months at Geneva, Blackwell was alternately elated and depressed. One diary entry, for example, reads, "Attended the demonstrator's evening lecture—very clear—how superior to books! Oh, this is the way to learn! The class behaves very well, and people seem all to grow kind." Another day, she was gloomy after helping Webster examine a female patient. "'Twas a horrible exposure; indecent for any poor woman to be subjected to such a torture," she wrote. "I felt more than ever the necessity of my mission," she added. "But I went home out of spirits. . . . I hardly know why. I felt alone. I must work by myself all life long."

When her first term ended, Blackwell returned to Philadelphia, where she spent the summer working at Blockley Almshouse, a charity hospital for the poor. The Blockley administrators were unenthusiastic about their new volunteer. They assigned her to a ward for women suffering from syphilis, a sexually transmitted disease. Blackwell's presence in "the most unruly part of the institution," they said, "might act as a check on the very disorderly inmates."

Delaware River boatmen bring supplies to Blockley Almshouse, the Philadelpha charity hospital where Blackwell interned in the summer of 1848.

The aspiring young doctor moved into her new quarters with characteristic calm. "My presence was a mystery to these poor creatures," she recalled. "I used to hear stealthy steps approach and pause at my door, evidently curious to know what I was about." Hoping to show the patients they had nothing to fear from her, she lined up her desk with the keyhole in her door. "There I worked," she said, "in view of any who chose to investigate the mysterious stranger." In a letter to her mother about life at Blockley, she wrote, "Do not fear for me. I go on smoothly and healthily. . . . I live simply, do my duty, trust in God, and mock at the devil!"

Blackwell's work among the syphilitic patients sparked a special, lifelong compassion for women suffering from venereal disease. The sick women she saw at Blockley had grown up in poverty. Uneducated and economically powerless, many had been victimized by the wealthy men in whose homes they worked as servants. "All this is horrible!" Blackwell wrote in her diary. "Women really must open their eyes to it. I am convinced that *they* must regulate this matter. But how?"

The hospital's chief physician liked Blackwell, but the young resident doctors—all male, of course—bitterly resented the presence of a female intern. "When I walked into wards they walked out," she noted. They also stopped filling out patients' charts when she was on duty, thus, as she said, "throwing me entirely on my own for clinical study." Nevertheless, she managed to write a medical paper on typhus, a deadly contagious disease whose victims crowded Blockley's wards.

In the mid-19th century, a doctor's education consisted of several years of private study followed by two years of medical school. Actual work with patients was not required; some doctors, in fact, entered their profession without ever having treated a human being. Blackwell, ahead of many of her classmates after her hands-on experience at Blockley, began her second and final term at Geneva College in October

1848. Surrounded by what she called "bright visions of usefulness," she worked harder than ever, her time "anxiously and engrossingly occupied with studies and the approaching examinations." Her social life, never active at Geneva, was now nonexistent. "I lived in my room and my college," she later recalled, "and the outside world made little impression on me."

At last it was time for final examinations. As she entered the room where the tests were given, she wrote later, "my face burned, my whole being was excited, but a great load was lifted from my mind." To no one's surprise, she received top honors in her class. To her own surprise, her fellow students showed no signs of envy. "I believe I shall receive my degree with their united approval," she confided in her diary.

To the young woman, graduation day was "bright and beautiful and very gratifying." After the ceremony, she wrote in her diary, "the audience applauded, but their presence was little

Dr. Benjamin Hale (above), president of Geneva Medical College, awarded Blackwell's diploma in 1849. When she received it, she said, she felt "angels" around her.

to me. I was filled with . . . high resolves for the future." It was January 23, 1849. "I felt the angels around me," wrote Elizabeth Blackwell, M.D.

Blackwell met Florence Nightingale, pictured above, in 1850. The two women, each determined to reform the medical profession, became lifelong friends.

FIVE

"Work On, Elizabeth!"

Blackwell was elated about receiving her medical degree, but she remained her usual, practical self. "I knew that a first step only had been taken," she wrote. "Much more medical experience than I possessed was needed." After graduation, she went back to Philadelphia, where she hoped to continue her studies. Soon after her arrival, she received a letter from her mother, who was more concerned about her daughter's spiritual condition than about her medical career.

"You urge upon me the importance of religion—why, bless the dear mother, what am I doing else but living religion all the time?" responded Blackwell. "I live in a good society, the fellowship of hard workers," she added. "I have the strengthening conviction that my aim is right, and that I, too, am working after my little fashion

for the redemption of mankind." Immensely pleased with her new title, she signed the letter "Your M.D."

Philadelphia's medical community greeted Blackwell politely. Even the University of Pennsylvania—which had refused her application two years earlier—honored her as a "professional sister." Nobody, however, offered her a job. "I am now longing to be at work abroad, where I can spend my time much more profitably," she wrote her mother. She decided that Paris, a hub of advanced medical activity, was the best place to complete her education. After "rubbing up" on her French, she paid a brief visit to her family in Cincinnati. She seemed "resolute in her course," noted her brother Samuel in his diary. But hers, he predicted, "will be a life of labor and self-sacrifice."

In April 1849 Blackwell sailed for

Even such ancient British monuments as St. Paul's Cathedral (seen here in 1848) seemed "new and striking" to Blackwell when she visited her native land in 1849.

England, where she planned to spend a few weeks before going to Paris. To the 28-year-old doctor, who had last seen her native land when she was 11, "everything seemed new and striking." She was enchanted by England's songbirds, its rolling green countryside, its "fresh and sweet" flowers. Like any other tourist, she visited castles, cathedrals, and London monuments. But most exciting were England's hospitals, where, to her surprise, she found herself something of a celebrity.

In a letter home, she reported that when one leading surgeon "found out I was really and truly a living woman, he sent me an invitation to the amputation he was about to perform." Although the chief physician at Birmingham's Lying-in (maternity) Hospital "thought that God and nature had indicated the unfitness of women for such a pursuit as I had chosen," he invited her to inspect his operating rooms. Each time she appeared at a British hospital, medical students crowded around her, excited about meeting the "daring little doctress from America."

Blackwell was enjoying England, but

"On May 31, 1849," Blackwell wrote in her autobiography, *"I found myself in the unknown world of Paris [above], bent upon the one object of pursuing my studies."*

she was eager to start her studies in Paris. By the end of May, full of high hopes, she was in the French capital. Her arrival had been marked by a minor misunderstanding, which she later recalled with amusement. Questioned about her occupation by a customs official, she responded with a word she thought meant *student*. "The man stared, and then standing in front of me began to make the most extraordinary grimaces, opening his eyes until the whites showed all around them," she wrote. Then, seeing her "look of astonishment," he tapped her gently on the shoulder and smiled. Surely madame had not meant to identify herself as a prostitute? Blackwell resolved to practice her French more diligently.

Paris, she remembered her medical teachers telling her, was the place where she would "find unlimited opportunities for study in any branch of the medical art." Bearing a letter of introduction from an American colleague, she sought out Pierre Louis, a prominent French physician. The distinguished-looking Louis listened impassively as she explained what she

Heating water on a woodstove, a midwife prepares to supervise the birth of a baby. For centuries, midwifery was the only branch of medicine open to women.

wanted: the chance to work in a Paris hospital under the supervision of experienced physicians. When she had finished, he looked at her coldly. Then he advised her to apply to La Maternité, a women's medical center where she could be trained as a midwife.

Louis had obviously assumed that, because of Blackwell's sex, her medical work would be limited to assisting women in childbirth. Blackwell recognized midwifery as an important part of the medical profession, but she had no intention of practicing it exclusively. She wanted to be a surgeon.

The director of the Paris hospital system refused to allow her to follow other doctors on their rounds, although this courtesy was routinely extended to male medical-school graduates. She was also barred from attending lectures at Paris's prestigious École de Médecine. One friendly physician made a familiar suggestion—that she attend the lectures disguised as a man—but she once again refused. She finally learned that the only Paris hospital that would admit her was La Maternité, the institution suggested by the disdainful Dr. Louis.

"The physicians of Paris," Blackwell wrote her mother, "are determined not to grant the slightest favor to a feminine M.D." Barred from conventional training, she decided to spend three months learning obstetrics, the branch of medical science concerned with childbirth. After that, she told her fam-

ily, "I shall try to accomplish my second object—surgery." In June 1849 she entered La Maternité, a huge institution surrounded by forbidding stone walls.

The hospital's program was rigorous. "Every moment of time was appropriated; no distractions of books, newspapers, or other than medical works were allowed; lectures, ward work, drills, and *cliniques* were arranged from morning till night," Blackwell told her family. Despite her medical degree, she enjoyed no special privileges. She slept in the same dormitory, ate in the same dining hall, and kept the same schedule as her fellow students, young women from the French provinces. She got along well with them, although at first, she noted, they were "much disappointed that I am not black, as they supposed all persons from America were!"

"How French girls do chatter!" Blackwell told her family. But she enjoyed the company of her high-spirited classmates, some of whom, she said, were "very pretty and graceful, some very rough." She also enjoyed the company of one of the interns, a handsome young man named Claude Hippolyte Blot. "I think he must be very *young*, or very much in awe of me," she told her mother, "for he never ventures to give me a direct look."

But before long, Blot found the courage to ask Blackwell to teach him English. The two young doctors (she was two years older than he) began to spend their free moments discussing medicine, philosophy, and their future careers. "I like him," Blackwell confided to her diary. "I hope we may come a little more closely together."

Like her classmates, Blackwell got up at 5:30 every morning, bathed and fed patients until 7:00, then reported to the wards, where she and the other trainees assisted the male resident doctors. Next came lectures on obstetrics, a hasty lunch, and a long period of work on the wards or in the delivery and operating rooms. Shifts varied from 12-hour days to 12-hour nights. It was a grueling schedule—Blackwell jokingly referred to herself as "the vol-

untary prisoner"—but she thrived on it. "Work on, Elizabeth!" she scribbled in her diary. At the end of the three months she had planned to spend at La Maternité, she signed up for an additional term. It was a decision that would have momentous—and heartbreaking—results.

In her journal, Blackwell noted that on November 4 she had "felt all the afternoon a little grain of sand, as it were, in one eye. I was afraid to think what it might be." Blackwell had good reason to be fearful. While cleaning the badly infected eye of an infant earlier in the day, she had accidentally splashed her own eye. Unable to open it the following day, she reported to

St. Bartholomew's Hospital, shown here, accepted Elizabeth Blackwell as an intern in 1850. She studied at the London institution for a year.

the infirmary, where her friend Dr. Blot was on duty.

He examined her eye carefully. Then he gave her bad news: She had contracted the disease, purulent ophthalmia, for which she had been treating the baby. Blot, Blackwell recalled later, "expressed much sympathy, arranged everything for me in the most thoughtful way, and I went to bed." The intern treated his patient with the latest medical procedures, which included applying extreme heat, ice, leeches, opium compresses, mustard plasters, and laxatives.

"My friendly young doctor came every two hours, day and night to tend the eye," wrote Blackwell. "For three days this continued—then the disease had done its worst.... Sight soon vanished, and the eye was left in darkness." Blackwell was ordered to stay in bed with both eyes bandaged for three weeks. When the bandages were removed, she could see light with her right eye. Vision in the left, however, was gone forever. Also gone was her dream of becoming the "first lady surgeon in the world."

Elizabeth Blackwell was not easily defeated. Soon after she left La Maternité, she wrote to relatives. "Fate certainly gave me a strange and sudden blow, but now I'm up again, strong and hopeful, and eager for work," she said. "In truth, dear friends, the accident might have been so much worse that I am more disposed to rejoice than to

To illustrate the danger of improper sanitation, a 19th-century cartoonist showed skeletal shopkeepers offering spoiled food and filthy clothing.

complain. Even in its present state the eye is not a very striking disfigurement, and it will gradually become still less so."

Meanwhile, Blot had received his diploma and opened a private practice. Blackwell had clearly enjoyed her association with him, but she had long ago decided she could not combine marriage and a medical career. "I shall miss him exceedingly when I leave [Paris]," she wrote her sister Emily, "for there is a most affectionate sympathy between us—but—a reformer's life is

"The Lady with the Lamp"—Florence Nightingale—checks wounded soldiers in a Crimean War hospital. Nightingale is known as the mother of modern nursing.

not a garden of roses." Her "beautiful friendship" with Blot, she decided firmly, would remain just that.

Six months after her illness had been diagnosed, Blackwell developed a severe inflammation in her blind eye. She had it removed by a surgeon, who replaced it with a glass eye. Then she took up where she had left off. During her convalescence, she had written to a British cousin, asking him to inquire about study opportunities in a London hospital. Her cousin's mission was successful: In mid-1850, she received a letter from the medical council of St. Bartholomew's, a large London hospital. "In the opinion of this committee," it stated, "Miss Blackwell should be admitted as a student."

Blackwell, said the hospital administrators, would be allowed to study in any ward and with any doctor willing to work with her. "This was indeed joyful news," Blackwell recalled in her autobiography. "I could now in an open and honorable way ... devote myself to the unlimited field of practical medicine." In October 1850 she left Paris, settled into a London boardinghouse, and reported for duty at St. Bartholomew's.

All the doctors "courteously welcomed me to their wards," she noted, "except the department for female diseases!" Ironically, the only medical field she had been allowed to study in Paris—obstetrics—was the only field closed to her in London. The head of the department told her he had nothing against her personally, but he could not give his approval to "a lady's studying medicine." Blackwell took his rejection philosophically. "A hundred years hence," she wrote her family, "women will not be what they are now."

Describing herself to her mother, Blackwell said that every morning, "a little dark figure with doctoral sack [loose black jacket] and writing case under arm makes its way through assembling students, who politely step aside to let it pass." She spent her days listening to lectures, watching operations, working with patients in the wards, and discussing cases with students and residents.

Her classmates, she said, were "gentlemanly," but they were not sure what to make of her. Some thought she was

"an extraordinary intellect," others regarded her as a "queer, eccentric woman." Blackwell wanted them to see her as she saw herself: "a quiet, sensible person who had acquired a small amount of medical knowledge, and who wished by patient observation and study to acquire considerably more." As time passed, her presence—and her solid determination—became familiar to the hospital staff. When she left the following year, one official delighted her by saying, "Why, we had quite forgotten you were here!"

During her year at St. Bartholomew's, Blackwell met several women who would become her lifelong friends. The first was Barbara Leigh Smith, a wealthy young painter and intellectual who would later spearhead the British feminist movement. Recognizing Blackwell as a kindred spirit, Smith invited her to gatherings where she met many of London's leading scientists, artists, and philosophers. Smith also introduced her cousin, Florence Nightingale, to the young doctor.

The daughter of a very well-to-do family, Nightingale was bored with her luxurious and unproductive existence. She had long dreamed of a career in public health, but her conservative relatives forbade it, considering such work "degrading." Deeply impressed by Blackwell's courage in entering the male-dominated medical profession, the 30-year-old Nightingale often visited her room. There the two women spent hours discussing nursing techniques, hospital reform, and the importance of sanitation in controlling the spread of disease and infections. Taken for granted today, scrupulous cleanliness in operating rooms and hospital wards was considered unnecessary by most doctors in the mid-19th century. To Nightingale, Blackwell later wrote, "I owed the awakening to the fact that sanitation is the supreme goal of medicine."

Blackwell and Nightingale often discussed the possibility of opening a hospital in which they could put their revolutionary ideas into effect. One day when Blackwell was visiting her friend at her country estate, Nightingale pointed at her family's huge mansion. "Do you know what I always think of when I look at that row of windows?" she asked. "I think how I should turn it into a hospital ward, and just how I should place the beds!"

The dreams of both women were to take real form. Nightingale would become known as "the Lady with the Lamp," world-famous for her heroic wartime nursing and her pioneering hospital reforms. And one day, not far in the future, Elizabeth Blackwell would establish her own hospital.

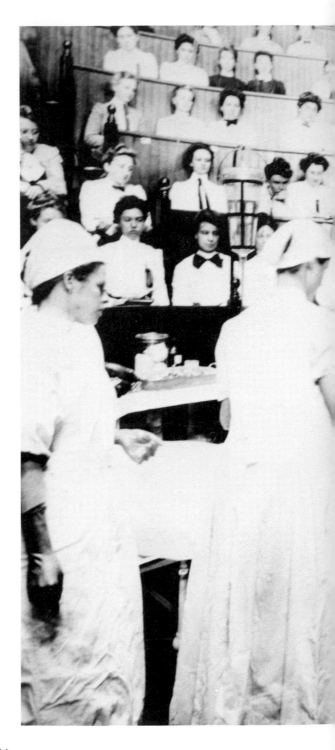

Observed by female medical students, women surgeons operate on a patient in 1903. Blackwell's pioneering work helped make such scenes possible.

Following in her older sister's footsteps, Emily Blackwell (above) decided to become a doctor. She graduated from Western Reserve Medical College in 1854.

S I X

"You Killed Her!"

After a year at St. Bartholomew's hospital, Elizabeth Blackwell was ready to head back to America to open her own office. When she thanked the hospital's officials for giving her permission to study at the institution, they issued a statement. "The result of such permission," it said, had "been most satisfactory." Blackwell had learned a great deal in London, and she had made many friends. But she was eager to start her medical practice in New York and to see her family, especially her 24-year-old sister, Emily.

Elizabeth Blackwell's graduation from medical school had broken down some of the prejudice against women as doctors. Now, two years later, U.S. medical colleges had accepted a few female students; among them was Emily Blackwell. "I wish I could lend you my little black stethoscope," said

Elizabeth when she heard the news. The two women decided to practice together after Emily's graduation.

Elizabeth told Emily about her dream of opening a hospital where she could experiment with new medical techniques. "If I were rich I would not begin private practice, but would only experiment," she wrote. "As, however, I am poor, I have no choice." She was eager to work with Emily and to share ideas with her. "I have really no *medical friend*," she said. "All the gentlemen I meet seem separated by an invincible, invisible barrier." But, she predicted, "it will not always be so. . . . Men and women will be valuable friends in medicine."

She arrived in New York in August 1851, ready to open an office and start seeing patients. Flushed with her success in London, she expected few

Tenement dwellers crowd a dark, littered courtyard in lower Manhattan. It was here that Blackwell opened her clinic for the poor in 1853.

she was a doctor in need of an office. Sometimes, the response was a simple no; more often, it was a door slammed in her face. Finally, one landlady agreed to accept her as a tenant, demanding an exorbitant rent and complaining bitterly about the M.D. sign Blackwell hung on her door. "Ladies would not reside in a house so marked," she sniffed.

Finding an office was only one of Blackwell's problems. She was often insulted in the streets, and other women sometimes moved aside when she passed, as though she carried a dangerous disease. She was even abused in writing: Her mail frequently contained anonymous obscene letters. She did her best to overlook these hostile acts. "With common sense, self-reliance, and attention to the work in hand," she said briskly, "any woman can pursue the medical calling without risk."

She decorated her new office, then sat down to wait for patients. None came. Deciding to establish a position with the local medical establishment, she brought her credentials to a city hospital. She would like to work, she said, as an assistant physician in the wards for women and children. The hospital administrators flatly turned her down, sarcastically suggesting that she open her own clinic. When she asked another hospital for permission to visit the women's wards, she received no answer at all.

problems. She was mistaken. To most New Yorkers of the time, a "female doctor" meant only one thing: an abortionist. Despite her proofs of bona fide medical training, Blackwell found landlords unwilling to rent office space to her.

She trudged through the streets for days, looking for "rooms to let" signs, ringing doorbells, and explaining that

"A blank wall of social and professional antagonism faces the woman physician," wrote Blackwell to her sister Emily. "[It] forms a situation of singular and painful loneliness." But Blackwell was not a woman to brood. Faced with empty hours and a vacant waiting room, she set to work writing a series of lectures on physical education for girls. When she finished them, she rented a church basement, ordered tickets printed, and placed a notice in the *New York Times*.

Blackwell's lectures would surprise no one today, but her words electrified what she called the "small but very

Members of an immigrant family gather in their squalid New York City apartment. Blackwell was especially concerned about the children of the poor.

intelligent audience of ladies" who heard them in the spring of 1852. The illnesses plaguing many women could be avoided, Blackwell said, if women better understood their own bodies. She discussed the importance of a balanced diet and adequate exercise, and she advised mothers to encourage their daughters to run, climb, ride horses, even wrestle. She also included a frank discussion of female anatomy and the birth process. "I think my writings belong to the year 1998," she joked.

After they recovered from their surprise at such candid remarks, Blackwell's listeners began to spread the word about her unconventional medical philosophy. By the end of the year,

Overflowing garbage barrels line a 19th-century Manhattan street. Such unsanitary conditions, Blackwell pointed out, contributed to the city's frequent epidemics.

her lectures had produced so much interest that a New York publisher arranged to print them under the title *The Laws of Life with Special Reference to the Physical Education of Girls*. The lectures also produced patients. Several of Blackwell's listeners engaged her as their family physician, and one prominent male doctor actually agreed to serve as her consultant. She wrote about this episode, which involved "a severe case of pneumonia in an elderly lady," in her autobiography.

"My first medical consultation was a curious experience," she recalled. After the doctor had examined the patient, he "began to walk about the room in some agitation, exclaiming, 'A most extraordinary case! ... I really do not know what to do!'" Blackwell was puzzled by the doctor's attitude, "as it was a clear case of pneumonia and of no unusual degree of danger." Finally, she said, she realized that "his perplexity related to *me*, not to the patient, and to the propriety of consulting with a lady physician!"

"Both amused and relieved," Blackwell told the doctor that if he was uneasy about their meeting, he could consider it "a friendly talk" instead of a professional consultation. The story had an upbeat ending: "He gave me his best advice; my patient rapidly got well, and happily I never afterwards had any difficulty in obtaining a necessary consultation from members of the profession."

By 1853 Blackwell had a few loyal patients, but she was not making enough money to live on. Once again, she tried to get a hospital job. Once again, she was bluntly refused. A woman doctor, said one hospital spokesman, "would not promote the harmonious working of the institution." If she wanted to help relieve human suffering, Blackwell finally concluded, she had only one choice: to open her own clinic. She resolved to found a dispensary where the poor could receive treatment and medicines at little or no cost. Borrowing money from friends, she rented a small office in the slums of lower Manhattan and announced that she would receive patients there three afternoons each week.

The New York Dispensary for Poor Women and Children filled a vital need for its poverty-stricken neighbors. It was soon crowded with patients, few of whom had ever seen a doctor before. Blackwell treated them in her office and in their squalid tenement rooms, delivering babies and attending sick children. She also gave advice about nutrition, the need for fresh air, and the importance of cleanliness. It was demanding, never-ending work, more than enough for a dozen Blackwells. By the summer of 1853, there were two: Emily, now a medical student, arrived to serve as assistant to her overworked sister. In the fall Emily headed west to study at Western Re-

After German-born Marie Zakrzewska (above) joined Blackwell at her dispensary in 1854, Blackwell taught her English and helped her get into medical school.

serve (now Case Western Reserve) Medical College in Cleveland, Ohio.

Meanwhile, the landlady at Blackwell's residence was becoming increasingly unpleasant. The high rent, too, was a heavy burden. Blackwell decided to buy a house; she would live in the attic, use one front room for an office, and rent out the rest for income. Choosing a large building on East 15th Street, she settled in and hung out her shingle, secure in the thought that no disapproving landlady could order her to remove it.

Children pray at a New York City orphanage. Visiting a similar institution in 1854, Blackwell met seven-year-old Kitty Barry, the Irish girl she later adopted.

After Emily Blackwell graduated with honors in early 1854, she followed her sister's footsteps to Europe, where she planned to study for two years. Soon after her arrival in Scotland, Emily received an excited letter from her older sister. Elizabeth said she had met a student who had "true stuff." Marie Zakrzewska (pronounced *zak-SHEF-ska*), a 24-year-old German-born Polish woman, had come to see her, seeking advice. The young woman, she told Blackwell, had been chief midwife at a large Berlin hospital. Forced to leave by staff members who were opposed to a woman holding such an important post, she had come to America to continue her medical training.

Zakrzewska spoke little English, but Blackwell knew enough German to communicate with her. After several hours of conversation, she was convinced that this young immigrant had a brilliant future, and she offered to teach her English and help her get into medical school. In the meantime, she could act as Blackwell's assistant at the busy dispensary. In her autobiography, published in 1924, Zakrzewska recorded her first impression of Blackwell:

She was a "rather short but stately lady, blond, with wavy hair, very dignified, kind in speech, and very deliberate and wise in her remarks," wrote Zakrzewska of her mentor. "I cannot comprehend how Dr. Blackwell could ever have taken so deep an interest in me," she continued. "She told me of her plan of founding a hospital—the long-cherished idea of my life—and said that she had opened a little dispensary . . . and she invited me to come and assist her. . . . The cordiality with which she welcomed me as a co-worker, I can never describe or forget. . . . All the days of disappointment were instantly forgotten."

For the next five months Zakrzewska worked with Blackwell, who arranged for her admission to Emily's alma mater, Western Reserve. In October the young woman left for Cleveland. After her departure, wrote Blackwell in her autobiography, "the utter loneliness of life became intolerable." She had long ago decided never to marry, but she yearned for companionship. Now she decided to adopt a little girl.

Hundreds of poor, orphaned children lived at the city's bleak immigrant depot. At this time, no laws or agencies regulating the placement of such children existed; any "respectable" person could visit the orphanage, sign a receipt, and take a child home. Arriving at the depot, Blackwell walked among throngs of children of all ages and nationalities. Some seemed healthy and cheerful; others were thin, shy, and forlorn. One of them, a frail girl with large, frightened eyes, particularly appealed to her. The matron in charge

Antoinette Brown (above) became America's first ordained female minister in 1853. Three years later, she married Elizabeth Blackwell's brother Sam.

was surprised. This child, she told Blackwell, was well behaved but "stupid," clearly not the best choice for adoption. "I thought otherwise," Blackwell recalled.

Born in Ireland, dark-haired Kitty

Feminist Lucy Stone (above) had vowed never to marry. Henry Blackwell changed her mind but not her name; after their 1855 wedding, she became "Mrs. Stone."

Barry was then about seven years old. "I chose her out of 400 children," Blackwell recalled later, "and she wanted to come with me.... I gave a receipt for her, and the poor little thing trotted after me like a dog." Blackwell wrote to her sister Emily about Kitty: "Instead of being stupid, I find now that she is withdrawn from blows and tyranny, that she is very bright.... She is not pretty, but has an honest little face ... and it is growing brighter every day under happier influences than the poor child has ever yet known." Not long afterward, Elizabeth Blackwell legally adopted Kitty Barry.

The two suited each other well. Blackwell gave Kitty the same kind of education she herself had received; Kitty in turn, helped around the house and was soon able to handle accounts for "Doctor," as she always called her adoptive mother. Each provided the other with the affectionate warmth she had been missing. In her autobiography, Blackwell recalled with amusement the day a male physician paid a call on her and Kitty. "After he was gone, she came to me with a very puzzled face, exclaiming, 'Doctor, how very odd it is to hear a *man* called Doctor!'"

On February 3, 1856, Blackwell made an entry in her diary. "My 35th birthday," she wrote. "On this bright Sunday morning I feel full of hope and strength for the future. Kitty plays beside me with her doll. She has just given me a candy basket purchased with a penny she earned, full of delight in Doctor's birthday! Who will ever guess the restoration and support which that poor forlorn little orphan has been to me! I desperately needed the diversion of thought she compelled me to give.... Heaven guide us all and make the gray hairs that are coming plentifully to me the sign of wisdom!"

Elizabeth Blackwell's "utter loneliness" would soon be only a memory. In the fall of 1856, she and Kitty were joined by a small army of Blackwells. Elizabeth's brother Sam had recently

Guests assemble for the 1857 launching of Blackwell's New York Infirmary for Indigent Women and Children. The clinic was staffed by female physicians.

married the Reverend Antoinette Brown, the first American woman to be ordained as a minister. Sam and his wife arrived for an extended visit to the house on 15th Street in October. Next came Hannah Blackwell and her daughters Ellen and Marian. A few months later, Elizabeth's brother Henry appeared with his wife, the celebrated feminist Lucy Stone. Stone had refused to change her name after her marriage, an act that inspired the term "Lucy Stoners" for married women who retained their maiden names.

Stone's gesture was admired by many people, including her husband, but Elizabeth Blackwell was not im-

pressed. She found it "a bit ridiculous" to refuse "to use the name of the man you had chosen in preference to that of a father you had *not* chosen." Nevertheless, she liked her new sister-in-law, and she greeted the whole clan with pleasure. "I have been more than eight years without a family circle," she wrote to Emily. "I can now appreciate one ... as I never did before."

A few months later, Emily added herself to the circle. "My working powers were more than doubled by the arrival of my sister," noted Elizabeth Blackwell. The household was completed with the arrival of Marie Zakrzewska, who had earned her medical

Henry Ward Beecher (above) delivered a stirring speech on the New York Infirmary's opening day. "Woman," he said, "has a right to do anything she can do well."

degree from Western Reserve. Dr. Elizabeth, Dr. Emily, and Dr. Zak, as the trio was sometimes known, now embarked on an intensive fund-raising campaign. They hoped to obtain enough money to realize their dream: a hospital run by women for women.

Getting support for the project was not easy. The women faced "a host of objections," Blackwell later recalled. They were told that no one would lease a house for such a purpose; that "female doctors would be looked upon with so much suspicion that the police would interfere"; that death certificates written by women physicians would not be legally valid; that patients could not be controlled without male resident doctors; "and finally, that they would never be able to collect money enough for so unpopular an undertaking."

The women physicians ignored these discouraging predictions. After a year of effort, much of it expended by the tireless "Dr. Zak," they had collected almost $5,000, enough to begin. They rented a house on Manhattan's Bleecker Street (now the center of Greenwich Village), and refitted it as a hospital, complete with two six-bed wards, an operating room, and a maternity floor. Wholesale druggists donated medicines for the dispensary, and supportive friends supplied linens and secondhand furniture.

The New York Infirmary for Indigent Women and Children formally opened on May 12, 1857. Elizabeth Blackwell had picked the date—Florence Nightingale's birthday—as a tribute to her friend, by now world-famous for her heroic work during the Crimean War. "The parlors were well filled with friends of the institution," reported the *New York Times*. Mingling with representatives from the Anti-Slavery Society and the Temperance Union were such prominent figures as clergyman Henry Ward Beecher (brother of novelist Harriet Beecher Stowe), and journalists Horace Greeley and James Gordon Bennett.

To mark the occasion, Beecher de-

An 1860 Harper's Weekly *illustration shows conditions that often prevailed in New York City hospitals. Blackwell was determined to eliminate such horrors.*

livered a resoundingly positive speech. "One day," he said, "it will be allowed by the reigning profession that woman was ordained to be a doctor. And when she has cured prejudice, she will have cured one of the very worst of the evils." Attacking the idea that women were best suited for such work as sewing, he said that "woman ... is peculiarly fitted for the study of medicine, and it is time she got away from the needle." Warming to his subject, he thundered, "I believe that little devil the needle has killed more women than any disease. Besides, woman has a right to do anything she can do well!"

When the men had finished speaking, Elizabeth Blackwell stepped forward. Those women who entered the medical profession, she said quietly, would have to be not only as good as men but better. The "education of women in medicine is a new idea, and like all other truths requires time to prove its value," she continued. And women, she insisted, "must prove their medical ability before expecting professional recognition." It was a surprisingly humble speech from a pioneer, but Elizabeth Blackwell knew that a whisper is sometimes more powerful than a shout.

Editor Horace Greeley scans a copy of his newspaper, the New York Tribune. *A strong supporter of Blackwell, he published many articles praising her work.*

"Whew! I hadn't calculated on a woman doctor!" says this male patient. Despite their progress, 19th-century female physicians were often ridiculed.

With Emily Blackwell as surgeon, Marie Zakrzewska as resident physician, and Elizabeth Blackwell as director, the infirmary began to serve patients. The three doctors spoke an array of foreign languages, useful in treating the German, Italian, and Slavic immigrants who crowded the waiting rooms and filled the beds. Although the hospital functioned smoothly from

the start, its success was punctuated by several alarming incidents. Zakrzewska wrote about one of them in her autobiography:

"A woman died in the hospital after childbirth. . . . It was not an hour after this sad occurrence before all the cousins who had relieved each other at the bedside appeared with their male cousins or husbands in working attire and with pickaxes and shovels ... demanding admission and shouting that the female physicians who resided within were killing women." Within minutes, continued Zakrzewska, "an immense crowd collected, filling the block ... howling and yelling and trying to push in the doors." As the mob shouted "You killed her!" the doctors did their best to calm their frightened patients, but they were surrounded, with no way to call for help.

At last, a burly Irish workman shoved his way to the top of the hospital steps and addressed the crowd. The "lady doctors," he said, we~ omen. They had saved ~ vn wife but the lives ~ of those present. At ~olicemen came rur ~ene. They

"ordered the crowd to disperse," recalled Zakrzewska, "telling them that they knew the doctors in that hospital treated the patients in the best possible way, and that no doctor could keep everybody from dying sometime." Its anger dissipated, the mob broke up and the hospital's tense occupants relaxed.

The New York Infirmary experienced several such incidents, but it flourished nonetheless. Existing records show that in the first 7 months of its operation, the Blackwells and Zakrzewska handled 645 medical, 227 gynecological, 36 surgical, and 18 obstetrical cases. These were the first of more than 1 million patients the infirmary would treat during the following 90 years.

Blackwell was 37 years old when she sat for this portrait. The female artist, noted one Blackwell biographer, was "charmed by her subject's delicate hand."

SEVEN

"Consider How Women Stand"

The New York Infirmary charged its patients $4 per week—if they could afford it. If not, treatment was free. Because most of the people who streamed into the hospital were poor, cash was always scarce. The women doctors still encountered flashes of hostility, but such occasions grew increasingly rare.

Meanwhile, Elizabeth Blackwell's British friends had been urging her to return to England. American women, they pointed out, had made great strides in medicine, thanks largely to Blackwell herself. Now it was time to move the battlefront to Great Britain, where progress for women was lagging far behind. As well as helping British women, Blackwell's friends pointed out, she could give lectures to raise funds for her hospital. In the summer of 1858 she decided to go, leaving the infirmary in the capable hands of her sister and Zakrzewska.

In August she and Kitty boarded the *Persia*, a large ocean liner powered by steam and sail, and set out for a year's stay in England. Blackwell, who had always suffered from seasickness, discovered that her daughter shared her problem. The two were violently ill all the way across the Atlantic. Nevertheless, 11-year-old Kitty was thrilled. "Ah, but she was a good ship!" she recalled. She and Blackwell visited friends and relatives in England and France, then settled in with Blackwell's sister Ellen, who was living in London.

Blackwell now began a whirlwind of activity. She revised her book, *The Laws*

In 1861, the Blackwells moved the New York Infirmary for Women and Children into new and larger quarters (above) on Manhattan's Second Avenue.

of Life, for British publication, visited hospitals, and gave speeches in hospitals, industrial centers, and public auditoriums across England. She insisted that women must understand the principles of health and the workings of the human body, and explained her theories on her profession. "What special contribution can women make to medicine?" she asked. "Not blind imitation of men ... for this would endorse the widespread error that the human race consists chiefly of men. Our duty is loyalty to right and opposition to wrong, in accordance with the essential principles of our own nature."

Blackwell's public appearances were greeted with contempt by some observers. One newspaper commented, "It is impossible that a woman whose hands reek with gore can be possessed of the same nature or feelings as the generality of women." Her lectures, however, were immensely popular among young women eager to enter the medical profession. One of them, Elizabeth Garrett, wrote to Blackwell six months after hearing her speak in London.

Garrett said Blackwell's words had provided her with "a strong conviction of [the medical profession's] fitness for women." Deciding to become a doctor, she had begun to study nursing, anatomy, and chemistry. Neither woman could know it at the time, of course, but Garrett would one day found England's first hospital for women and would work with Blackwell to erect another milestone in medical history.

While she was in England, Blackwell renewed her friendship with Florence Nightingale, by now celebrated as a pioneering hospital reformer as well as a courageous wartime nurse. Nightingale, who was independently wealthy, told Blackwell that she planned to establish a training school for female nurses, the first of its kind in the world. The perfect director for the school, she added, would be Elizabeth Blackwell. Although she admired her friend's energy and vision, Blackwell declined. She had fought too hard for the right to practice medicine to give it up, even for a project as worthy as Nightingale's.

Nightingale was not alone in urging

Blackwell to remain in England. Scores of prominent women—and men—tried to persuade her to stay and help British women gain a foothold in medicine. Blackwell, however, was anxious to return to New York and her infirmary. To one of her British supporters she wrote, "The children of the present generation will grow up accustomed to women doctors, respecting and trusting them.... I shall go back to create the institutions of which we have planted only the little germ."

Blackwell's thoughts about returning to the United States were crystallized by a letter she received in June 1859: Marie Zakrzewska had accepted a job as professor of obstetrics at a Boston college. Blackwell, who had expected her protégé to leave after two years' service at the infirmary, approved of the move, but she knew her sister could not run the infirmary single-handedly. It was time to go home. When she and her daughter returned to the United States in July, she brought with her a large cash contribution from a French admirer. She also carried a certificate of enrollment in the British Medical Register, which made her the first woman so honored.

In New York, Blackwell plunged back into hospital and private practice. "How good work is—work that has a soul in it!" she wrote to a friend in England. "I cannot conceive that anything can supply its want to a woman.... True work is perfect freedom." The infirmary had prospered during her absence, and its trustees had raised enough money to buy a permanent site. Elizabeth and Emily Blackwell soon found an ideal building for the hospital, a large structure on Manhattan's Second Avenue. Elizabeth sold the house on 15th Street and, with her sister and Kitty, moved into the new building. Then she began to campaign for her next goal: a medical school for women, to be attached to the New York Infirmary.

By now a confident public speaker, Blackwell captured audiences with her appeals. The college she envisioned, she said, would "widen women's sphere, link science with their everyday life, bring them into closer touch with the world around them." In deference to convention she added, "and make them better mothers." She asked her listeners to "help us to build up a noble institution for women—such an institution as no country has ever yet been blessed with, a national college hospital in which all parts of the Union shall join."

The Union, however, was in danger. On April 12, 1861, the first shots of the Civil War were fired at Fort Sumter, South Carolina. Plans for the "college hospital" would have to wait until the crisis was over. Both North and South were soon on the march, sending thousands of men into some of the bloodiest battles ever fought. As the

Union soldiers defend Fort Sumter on April 12, 1861. The South Carolina battle marked the start of the Civil War, which was to rage for the next four years.

staggering casualty reports rolled in, Elizabeth Blackwell knew that nurses would be needed immediately. Many people believed that women—the "weaker sex"—had no place at the front, but Blackwell thought differently. She mobilized for action, first calling an emergency meeting at the infirmary.

To her surprise, a huge crowd showed up. There was "a perfect mania among the women," she recalled, "to act 'Florence Nightingale!'" Clearly, the work to be done required larger facilities than the infirmary could handle. The next meeting, held in New York's vast Cooper Institute, drew almost 4,000 people, all of them eager to aid Union troops. Organized at this session was the Women's Central Relief Association, which became responsible for supplying nurses for the army. Blackwell, who was appointed head of the registration committee, now divided her long working days between the infirmary and the Cooper Institute, where she interviewed volunteers, selected candidates, and sent them to New York Hospital or to her own infirmary for a month's training.

The women chosen to serve as nurses faced grueling action. In her autobiography, Blackwell wrote about one "feeble-looking" individual she had almost rejected. After the Battle of Gettysburg, a pivotal contest fought in Pennsylvania in July 1863, Blackwell admiringly reported that this frail

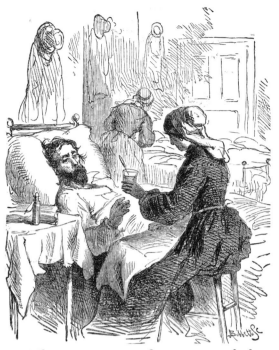

A Civil War nurse comforts a wounded Union soldier. Blackwell spent the war years recruiting and training nurses as well as running her own hospital.

nurse "spent two days and nights on the field of slaughter, wading with men's boots in the blood and mud, pulling out the still living bodies from the heaps of slain, binding up hideous wounds, giving a draught of water to one, placing a rough pillow under the head of another, in an enthusiasm of beneficence which triumphed . . . over thought of self." So much, Elizabeth Blackwell must have thought, for the "weaker" sex!

Meanwhile, business at the infirmary was booming. In 1860 the Blackwell sisters and their assistants treated

Union soldiers lie dead after the Battle of Gettysburg, fought in July 1863. Almost 50,000 men were killed or wounded during the fierce three-day conflict.

3,680 patients; two years later, the patient total was a stunning 6,872. Dedicated abolitionists, the Blackwells had always treated the needy of all races at the hospital. Their enlightened attitude brought them close to disaster in the summer of 1863, when long-simmering resentment against the war came to a boil.

In July the federal government announced plans to draft soldiers into the army, sparking a wave of violence known as the Draft Riots. Murderous mobs surged through the streets of New York City, looting, setting fires, and hunting down the people they held responsible for the war: blacks

and abolitionists. Inside the infirmary, white patients demanded the ejection of blacks, whose presence might bring on the fury of the mobs outside. Elizabeth Blackwell and her sister, predictably, refused to betray their black patients.

For three sleepless days and nights, the Blackwells paced the wards, comforting the sick as the city rocked with screams and explosions. On the next block, an entire row of houses went up in flames; the doctors calmly shielded the eyes of terrified patients. Miraculously, none of the rioters seemed to remember that the New York Infirmary harbored both highly suspect "doctresses" and blacks. When the savagery ended, the infirmary was intact, its patients and staff unharmed. Characteristically, Elizabeth Blackwell had remained calm and steady throughout the nightmare. Also characteristically, she never even mentioned it in her autobiography.

In April 1865 the Confederacy surrendered to the Union, ending four years of war. Elizabeth Blackwell could now take up where she had left off: expanding the work of the infirmary. Convinced that preventing disease was as important as treating it, she had long wanted to employ a "sanitary inspector." The inspector, a forerunner of the district nurse and public health worker, would visit the homes of the infirmary's poor outpatients, few of whom understood the basics of good health practice. As well as explaining the importance of cleanliness, fresh air, exercise, and proper nutrition, the inspector would give lessons on infant care. Blackwell was particularly eager to improve the health of the babies born to the city's poor. "Children," she insisted, "are born to live, not die."

In 1866 a supporter's donation enabled her to realize her wish. She engaged a series of health inspectors who fanned out into the slums, bringing soap, disinfectants, and pamphlets on health care, which they often read aloud to illiterate families. By 1872 the infirmary was fielding a team of inspectors, headed by Dr. Rebecca Cole, America's first black woman physician. Cole served as chief inspector for 9 years, during which she and her assistants made 10,442 outpatient visits.

Blackwell's next project was the establishment of the infirmary's medical

Second Avenue, site of the Blackwells' infirmary, was the scene of a bloody confrontation during the Draft Riots that swept New York City in 1863.

Dr. Rebecca Cole (standing), America's first black female doctor and the New York Infirmary's chief sanitary inspector, attends a hospital staff meeting.

college. In 1864 New York State had empowered the institution "to grant and confer the title of Doctor of Medicine." But Blackwell was unable to put that power to practical use until the war was over and the necessary funds were raised. Finally, by early 1868, she and her supporters had collected almost enough money, much of it donated by people who had listened to her personal appeals.

"The practice of medicine by women," she would say, "is no longer a doubtful but a settled thing." However, she would add, "Consider how women stand in this matter; how alone, how unsupported; no libraries, museums, hospitals, dispensaries, clinics; no endowments, scholarships, professorships, prizes, to stimulate and reward study; no time-honored institutions and customs, no recognized position; no societies, meetings, and professional companionship. One can hardly conceive of more complete isolation."

On November 2, 1868, after 15 years of effort, Blackwell presided over the opening of the Women's Medical College of the New York Infirmary. "It is an

Manhattan slum residents chat with a visiting nurse in 1910. The city's public-health system began with the sanitary inspectors Blackwell dispatched in 1865.

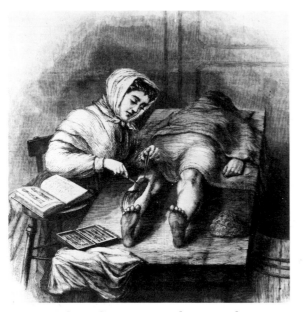

A student dissects a cadaver at the Women's Medical College. Established in 1868, the school was one of Blackwell's greatest triumphs.

easy thing to found a poor college," she said. "To found a really good college is a work of great difficulty." The women's college, she explained, would break new ground. Unlike most existing medical schools, it would establish stiff entrance requirements, require 3 years—instead of the standard 10 months—of classroom training, provide graded courses and clinical experience, and appoint an independent examining board to grant diplomas.

Blackwell could hardly believe that the great day had arrived at last. "We are so accustomed to be despised and rejected that encouragement, welcome, success, seem unaccountable,"

she said. "It is like breathing a new and delightful atmosphere, which is, nevertheless, strange and dreamlike; and one almost fears to wake up with a shock."

No shock, however, was in store for Blackwell. The school began with 17 women students and 11 professors and instructors. Elizabeth Blackwell taught her favorite subject, hygiene; her sister acted as professor of obstetrics and women's diseases. Serving on the faculty along with the women were several prominent men, including Elizabeth Blackwell's classmate at Geneva College, Stephen Smith, now a celebrated New York physician.

"In 1869, the early pioneer work in America was ended," observed Blackwell in her autobiography. "In Boston, New York, and Philadelphia, special medical schools for women were sanctioned by the legislatures, and in some long-established colleges, women were received as students in the ordinary classes." Furthermore, the infirmary and college Blackwell had built were running smoothly under the skillful management of Emily Blackwell. "She does grandly as the center of this movement—towers a head and shoulders above her students, who have immense confidence in her," said Elizabeth Blackwell of her sister.

Ongoing progress for women physicians seemed assured in the United States. In England, however, it had reached an impasse. After a long strug-

Fulfilling Blackwell's dream, the first graduates of the Women's Medical College of the New York Infirmary receive their diplomas.

gle, Elizabeth Garrett had finally gotten her medical degree in 1862, becoming the second woman—after Elizabeth Blackwell—to be listed in the British Medical Register. But following her certification, Garrett's male colleagues had closed ranks against women. Once again, Blackwell's English friends were clamoring for her presence. "Come to England," said one letter. "We need you desperately. Come and help us do for the women of England what you have done for the women of America."

Blackwell rose to the challenge. As always, she needed new battles to fight, new frontiers to cross. Only 48 years old, she had plenty of energy; many productive years still lay ahead. "It's my nature to start anew," she wrote. "What is done is done. I will leave it." In July 1869 she once again set out for England.

The outspoken Blackwell once joked that her writings "belonged to the year 1998." As she aged, her blunt observations continued to shock the straitlaced.

EIGHT

"She Conquered So Much"

When Blackwell returned to England in 1869, she hoped "both to renew physical strength, which had been severely tried, and to enlarge [her] experience of life." But she said her main purpose in going was to assist other female physicians "in the pioneer work so bravely commencing." She rented a house in London and started to practice medicine. Then she sent for 23-year old Kitty Blackwell. "You can help me so much," she told "Kittykin," as she called her daughter, "by taking charge of my things and telling me where they are; and reading and occasionally stitching for me . . . and above all loving me very much."

Just before Kitty joined her in London in September 1870, Blackwell received sad news from home: Her mother had died at the age of 77. Hannah Blackwell, mother of two pioneering female doctors, mother-in-law of two influential feminists, was widely mourned. "In the best sense of the word," said one obituary notice, "she was a constructive radical."

Blackwell grieved for her mother, but, as usual, she concentrated on the present rather than the past. She was soon back on the lecture platform, airing her views on such pet subjects as hygiene and nutrition. She also discussed family planning and sex education for children, highly controversial subjects in Victorian England. One of her lectures, entitled "How to Keep a Household in Health," stirred up a hornet's nest.

After the speech was reported, London newspapers were flooded with letters from outraged readers. One writer, who signed herself "A Brooding Hen," called Blackwell a member of

British coal miners fight for their lives after a mine-shaft accident. Blackwell campaigned vigorously for laws to protect such endangered workers.

ously for laws against polluted water supplies, overcrowded and airless tenements, and hazardous working conditions, particularly in England's notoriously dangerous coal mines. "We now possess enough sanitary knowledge to reform the physical and moral condition of the human race," she asserted, adding that proper sanitary procedures "would save the lives of tens of thousands of human beings around us . . . and make our homes the precious centers of ennobling influence that they are intended to be."

In 1871 Blackwell and her allies formed the National Health Society. Dedicated to "the promotion of health among all classes of the population," the organization adopted one of Blackwell's trademark phrases as its motto: "Prevention is better than cure." It began educating the public about little-understood hygienic practices, holding classes for mothers, and training volunteer health workers. Blackwell called the society "an architecture of the future, for the benefit of generations to come." Created by a small group of reformers, the National Health Society would become a large, highly influential body, shaping British public-health policies for generations. Its governing board eventually included members of Britain's royal family, high-ranking church officials, and representatives of the nation's professions.

Although not everyone in England

"the shrieking sisterhood." Another warned that her advice about limiting the size of families would result in a wave of infanticide (the killing of children). Blackwell also received stacks of abusive mail at home. But none of this was new to the outspoken doctor. She kept right on lecturing.

Sanitation, she insisted, was the key to good health. She campaigned vigor-

Slum dwellers congregate in a filthy London alley. Lack of sanitation, Blackwell insisted, resulted in the loss of thousands of lives each year.

Inspired to become a doctor by Blackwell, Elizabeth Garrett faces the Paris board of medical examiners. She earned her medical degree in 1870.

agreed with Blackwell's ideas, she was respected for her sincerity and dogged persistence. Tirelessly arguing the case for women doctors, she gradually chipped away at the British medical profession's deep opposition to admitting women to its ranks. The first to break through had been Elizabeth Garrett, the young woman who was inspired to study medicine when she heard Blackwell speak in 1859.

Another Blackwell protégé, Sophia Jex-Blake, had enrolled in the New York Infirmary Medical College in 1869 but had been called home by a family emergency. She managed to attend medical classes at the University of Edinburgh the following year, but she was prevented from graduating by violent opposition from male students. She had obtained her medical degree in Switzerland and, with the aid of Blackwell and Garrett, founded the London School of Medicine for Women in 1874.

Blackwell accepted the post of professor of gynecology at the new school. She considered it a "privilege and pleasure," she said modestly, "in some small degree to encourage these brave workers in their pioneer enterprise." Her direct connection with the school, however, was not to last. She had been plagued for some time with a painful condition she called "biliary colic," probably a liver ailment. Writing to a friend in 1876, she said, "I have been really ill for the last month in London—13 attacks of hours of agonizing pain and vomiting." By the time she had finished one semester of lecturing at the London School of Medicine, she realized "with bitter disappointment" that she would have to take some time off from her duties.

Hoping that a change of climate would improve matters, she and Kitty went to Italy. The warm Italian sunshine was helpful, but Blackwell was restless, uneasy about abandoning what she called her "medical responsibility." In the winter of 1876, she addressed the problem by writing a book. "Under the olive trees," she recalled in her autobiography, "I meditated on the duty of the physician, and finally wrote the small work, *Counsel to Parents on the Moral Education of Their Children*." The book may have been small, but it was a bombshell.

Counsel to Parents, a guide to sex education for young people, would shock no one today. Still, Blackwell's relatively frank language was ahead of its time. She showed the manuscript to a literary friend who, she recalled later, "assured me that if I published, my name would be a forbidden word in England." Undaunted, she sent the book to 12 London publishers. Each quickly rejected it. At last, it reached an editor who wanted to release it, but

he had reckoned without his firm's senior partner: The work, declared the pious partner, was unprintable.

The resourceful editor, who strongly believed that *Counsel to Parents* should be published, suggested that it be submitted to a group of clergymen for their opinion. After much discussion, a decision was reached: The book would appear, but as a medical work, and it would have a solemn new title, *The Moral Education of the Young, Considered Under the Medical and Social Aspects*. "Looking at the very reticent [reserved] way in which the

Blackwell disciple Sophia Jex-Blake (above) graduated from a Swiss medical college. In 1874 she founded the London School of Medicine for Women.

Elizabeth and Kitty Blackwell moved to Rock House (above) in 1879. The 2 women lived in the cliffside cottage for the next 30 years.

subject is treated in this little book," mused Blackwell later, "it is difficult to believe that such an episode could have occurred."

The public turned out to be less easily offended than the publishing industry. Blackwell's book was a resounding success, reprinted several times in England and, in 1879, published in the United States under its original title. "Coming from a woman," said the *New York Star*, "this book is unique, but its testimony is so bravely given . . . that it must be welcomed by all sincere moral workers as one of the ablest appeals in behalf of chastity and sexual nobility of life."

Soon after Blackwell's 58th birthday

in 1879, she and Kitty moved into "Rock House," a British seaside cottage. Perched on a high cliff overlooking the English Channel, Rock House would be home to the doctor and her daughter for the next three decades. Here Blackwell would study, write books and pamphlets, plan reform campaigns, and entertain family and friends. Among the first callers at Rock House was Dr. Marie Zakrzewska. She and Blackwell had kept up their friendship by mail, but this was their first meeting in years.

"Dr. Zak" delighted her mentor with stories about the New England Hospital for Women and Children, which she had founded in Boston in 1862.

Dedicated to the training of women doctors and nurses, the New England Hospital had established high standards and greatly strengthened public acceptance of female physicians. Her friend's progress, said Blackwell, was "quite encouraging."

Blackwell would spend her years at Rock House working for a dazzling array of medical, social, and moral causes. Some of her ventures were successful, some not. Among the failures was her effort to establish a woman's agricultural college. Few of her allies, she discovered, shared her belief that farming would be an ideal occupation for women. More rewarding was her passionate campaign against vivisection, experimental surgery performed on living, conscious animals. Convinced that such experimentation was cruel and immoral, Blackwell denounced it in speeches and pamphlets. Although legislation regulating the treatment of laboratory animals would not be enacted until many years after her death, her crusade helped to make it possible.

Another issue that ignited Blackwell's fury was prostitution, which she regarded as an "unmitigated evil." Society, she pointed out, expected "respectable" women to be moral but made no such demands on men. She demanded a single standard for both sexes—not equal sexual freedom, but equal sexual restraint. Particularly irritating to Blackwell were laws that punished the prostitute but not the men who paid for her services. "Those who make the trade profitable," she said, "are not less guilty and degraded than the women whom they subject to scorn." Joining forces with other reform-minded women and men, she pressed for legal changes and, as usual, made her ideas widely known through speeches and such publications as 1883's *Wrong and Right Methods of Dealing with Social Evil.*

When Marie Zakrzewska (above) visited Blackwell at Rock House, the old friends discussed both the past and the future. Women, they agreed, had come a long way.

A prostitute waits for customers outside a rooming house. The reform of British laws dealing with prostitution was high on Blackwell's list of priorities.

As the years passed, Blackwell continued to study, lecture, and write. At Kitty's request, she started an autobiography in 1887. Filled with comments, letters, and diary extracts, the book was published in 1895 under the title *Pioneer Work in Opening the Medical Profession to Women*. Blackwell's original manuscript included a dedication to Kitty. "I should hardly care to [write this]," it said, "if I were not prompted by my affection for you; for

as I draw near the borderland, the individual life seems so small in comparison with the grand whole. . . . The little unknown child, whom I took to myself 33 years ago, at a very dreary time in my life, and whom I carried up to bed in my arms—has proved a real daughter to me; and this record shall be a legacy of my affection to her."

Kitty Blackwell, "the little unknown child," was 48 years old when her adoptive mother's memoirs were published. Although she had weak eyesight and was somewhat hard of hearing, she was a lively, intelligent, and attractive woman. But like Elizabeth, Anna, Marian, Emily, and Ellen Blackwell, she never married. Apparently, she was well satisfied with her role as devoted daughter, secretary, and companion to her beloved "Doctor."

Elizabeth Blackwell had written of herself as being near death's "borderland" in 1887, but she had many productive years ahead of her, and she outlived most of her friends and relatives. Her sister-in-law, women's rights crusader Lucy Stone, died in 1893, novelist Harriet Beecher Stowe in 1896. Soon afterward, Blackwell lost her brother Samuel and her sisters Anna, Ellen, and Marian. Marie Zakrzewska, 72, died in 1902; as she had directed, her own words were read at her funeral service. Among them was a tribute to her mentor. "Dr. Elizabeth Blackwell," she had written, "has been the most powerful agent in strengthening what was weak in me."

Blackwell gave up her private medical practice in 1894. In her diary, she crisply noted the reason: At 73, she feared she could no longer "supply the magnetism that I have always given to my patients." A resolute diarist since childhood, she never abandoned the habit. On February 3, 1900, she wrote, "My birthday, 79 years old—physically I feel my advancing years—but spiritually it seems to me the outlook becomes increasingly wider and brighter as to the future." Still to come were more books, more lectures, more crusades for the causes she believed in: birth control, sex education for the young, the elimination of prostitution, the need for women physicians.

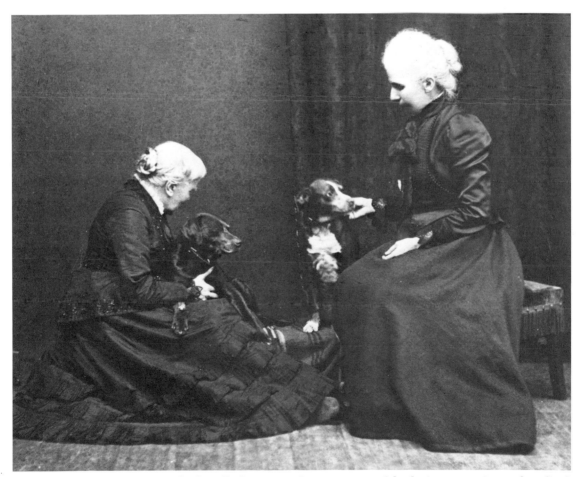

Elizabeth (left) and Kitty Blackwell share a quiet moment with their pets. Kitty, who died in 1936, spent her last years with Henry Blackwell's daughter Alice.

Still going strong at 85, Blackwell visited the United States with her daughter in the summer of 1906. Aware that she was seeing most of them for the last time, she had a happy reunion with her surviving siblings and her numerous nieces and nephews. "She had a firm nose, mouth, and chin, a very vivacious expression, and a charming manner," recalled one niece later. "She had a sense of fun, but she had masterful persistence when she felt she was right." Although she found her Aunt Elizabeth "sweet and serene," added the niece, "I stood in awe of her. One felt she had conquered so much."

Elizabeth and Kitty Blackwell spent the following summer at their favorite retreat, a small hotel in the Scottish mountain village of Kilmun. Here Blackwell suffered a disastrous fall, plunging headlong down a flight of stairs at the inn. She never truly recovered from the accident. Her once-alert mind vague, her eternal vigor drained, she spent the next three years in an almost dreamlike state, silent and withdrawn. With Kitty at her side, Elizabeth Blackwell died peacefully on May 31, 1910.

Blackwell had long ago said she would like to be buried at Kilmun, and it was there that Kitty laid her to rest under a white stone cross. Engraved on the simple monument were words that Blackwell would probably have approved: "The first woman of modern times to graduate in medicine (1849) and the first to be placed on the British Medical Register (1859)."

British and American newspapers printed long, respectful accounts of Blackwell's life and death. Summing

Blackwell's grave in Scotland records her proudest accomplishment: "The First Woman of Modern Times to Graduate in Medicine."

The institution founded by Elizabeth Blackwell, now called New York Infirmary-Beekman Downtown Hospital, occupies a large, modern building in lower Manhattan.

them up was a comment in the London *Times*: "She was in the fullest sense of the word a pioneer." Another publication pointed out a statistic that would have pleased Blackwell even more: By 1910, there were 7,399 woman doctors registered in the United States alone. And 75 years later, at the end of 1985, the American Medical Association listed 80,725 woman doctors. In one sense, each was a daughter of Elizabeth Blackwell.

FURTHER READING

Abram, Ruth J. *"Send Us a Lady Physician": Women Doctors in America, 1835–1920*. New York: Norton, 1985.

Baker, Rachel. *The First Woman Doctor*. New York: Scholastic, 1961.

Blackwell, Elizabeth. *Pioneer Work in Opening the Medical Profession to Women: Autobiographical Sketches*. New York: Source Book Press, 1970.

Ehrenreich, Barbara, and Deirdre English. *For Her Own Good: 150 Years of the Experts' Advice to Women*. Garden City, NY: Anchor Press/Doubleday, 1978.

Forster, Margaret. *Significant Sisters: The Grassroots of Active Feminism*. New York: Oxford University Press, 1984.

Hays, Elinor Rice. *Those Extraordinary Blackwells*. New York: Harcourt Brace Jovanovich, 1967.

Johnston, Malcolm Sanders. *Elizabeth Blackwell and Her Alma Mater*. Geneva, NY: W. F. Humphrey Press, 1947.

Pfeiffer, Carl J. *The Art and Practice of Western Medicine in the Early Nineteenth Century*. London: McFarland, 1985.

Ross, Ishbel. *Child of Destiny: The Life Story of the First Woman Doctor*. New York: Harper & Row, 1949.

Rothstein, William G. *American Physicians in the 19th Century: From Sects to Science*. Baltimore, MD: Johns Hopkins University Press, 1972.

Sahli, Nancy Ann. *Elizabeth Blackwell, M.D. (1821–1910), a Biography*. Salem, NH: Arno, 1982.

Shyrock, Richard Harrison. *Medicine in America: Historical Essays*. Baltimore, MD: Johns Hopkins University Press, 1966.

Wilson, Dorothy Clarke. *Lone Woman: The Story of Elizabeth Blackwell*. Boston, MA: Little, Brown, 1970.

CHRONOLOGY

Feb. 3, 1821	Elizabeth Blackwell born in Bristol, England
1832	Emigrates to America with family; settles in New York City
1838	Moves to Cincinnati, Ohio; father dies; the Blackwell sisters open a boarding school
1844	Takes teaching job in Henderson, Kentucky
1845	Decides to become a doctor; teaches school and studies medicine in Asheville, North Carolina
1847	Moves to Philadelphia; after 28 medical school rejections, accepted at Geneva (New York) Medical College
1848	Spends summer working in women's syphilitic ward in Blockley Almshouse in Philadelphia
1849	Graduates from Geneva at the head of her class; goes to Paris; interns at La Maternité, a woman's hospital; contracts eye disease leading to loss of left eye
1850	Joins staff of St. Bartholomew's Hospital in London as an intern; meets Florence Nightingale
1851	Returns to New York to open private medical practice
1852	Delivers series of lectures on female health
1853	Opens Manhattan clinic for poor women and children
1854	Meets future doctor and medical partner, Marie Zakrzewska; adopts Kitty Barry, a seven-year-old Irish orphan
1858	Departs for yearlong fund-raising trip to England; becomes first woman listed in British Medical Register
1861	Organizes Civil War nursing service
1866	Establishes first visiting-nurse program (New York City)
1868	Opens Women's Medical College in New York City, first such institution in history
1869	Returns to England to aid British women's struggle to enter field of medicine
1870	Helps found British National Health Society
1876	Teaches gynecology at newly established London School of Medicine for Women; Publishes *The Moral Education of the Young* (*Counsel to Parents*)
1894	Retires from medical practice; continues to lecture and write pamphlets on social and medical issues
1895	Publishes autobiography, *Pioneer Work in Opening the Medical Profession to Women*
1906	Makes last visit to the United States
May 31, 1910	Dies of a stroke at the age of 89

INDEX

INDEX

PICTURE CREDITS

Archives and Special Collections on Women in Medicine, Medical College of Pennsylvania: pp. 22, 65, 66, 101;   The Bettmann Archive: pp. 17, 21, 24, 28, 30, 34, 35, 36, 39, 40, 41, 46, 47, 48, 49, 56, 58, 60, 62, 63, 64, 70, 71, 72, 74, 80, 88, 89, 91, 92, 93, 96, 97, 98;   Cincinnati Historical Society: p. 32;   Culver Pictures: pp. 15, 18, 20, 25, 26, 27, 31, 38, 42, 43, 54, 59, 78, 79, 80, 84, 85, 87, 102;   Geneva Historical Society: pp. 14, 55;   Harcourt Brace Jovanovich: p. 19;   Hobart and William Smith Colleges: pp. 44, 51;   Lane Theological Seminary: p. 37;   The Library of Congress: p. 90;   National Library of Medicine: p. 99;   New York Academy of Medicine Library: pp. 50, 52;   New York Infirmary, Beekman Downtown Hospital: pp. 12, 77, 94, 105;   Schlesinger Library, Radcliffe College: pp. 2, 16, 73, 75, 82, 100, 103;   Sophia Smith Collection, Smith College: pp. 68, 76;   The Welfare History Picture Library, The Heatherbank Museum of Social Work: p. 104

Jordan Brown holds a bachelor's degree in English from Bennington College and is presently enrolled in the graduate writing program at Sarah Lawrence College. She brings to the subject of Elizabeth Blackwell a special interest in health and women's history.

❖   ❖   ❖

Matina S. Horner is president of Radcliffe College and associate professor of psychology and social relations at Harvard University. She is best known for her studies of women's motivation, achievement, and personality development. Dr. Horner serves on several national boards and advisory councils, including those of the National Science Foundation, Time Inc., and the Women's Research and Education Institute. She earned her B. A. from Bryn Mawr College and Ph.D. from the University of Michigan, and holds honorary degrees from many colleges and universities, including Mount Holyoke, Smith, Tufts, and the University of Pennsylvania.